THE
T☣XIC
FAMILY
SOLUTION

**Surviving Your Toxic Family &
Reclaiming Your Life After Toxic Parents**

STEVEN TODD BRYANT

DISCLAIMER

This book is not intended as a substitute for the medical advice of physicians. The reader must consult a physician in matters relating to his/her/their health and particularly with respect to any symptoms that may require diagnosis or medical attention. Although the author has made every effort to ensure the information in this book was correct at press time, the author does not assume and hereby disclaims any liability to any party for any loss, damage, or disruption caused by errors or omissions for any reason. The author cannot be held legally responsible for any damages suffered because of this publication or the content of 3rd party web pages or resources. In some cases, stories have been fictionalized, and names and identifying details have been omitted or changed to protect the privacy of individuals.

CONTENTS

— ❧ —

THERAPIST RECOMMENDED

"Fantastic! I wish I had read this book 30 years ago when I first started my practice. *The Toxic Family Solution* conveys complex concepts in a manner that is easy to understand for both novices and the experienced alike. It is chock full of examples, stories, and direction, all designed to ease you into a meditative practice. It's a pragmatic guide that empowers the reader with mindfulness concepts and resources." - William E. Range MC, LMHC, Licensed Therapist

"*The Toxic Family Solution* provides readers with a roadmap to move forward from family trauma and suffering. Steven's experiences highlight the unhealthy identity development many struggle with when growing up in a toxic family. We don't get to choose which families we are born into, and an abusive home environment can be extremely detrimental to our personal development. However, with the right toolkit, we can develop our own authentic selves. The lessons and skills that Steven highlights can help any survivor of a toxic family take positive steps toward personal fulfillment. Wherever you are in your journey following a painful home life, this book can help you move forward and make peace with your life." - Caleb Sheldrup, M. Psych.

DEDICATION

For Efren

INTRODUCTION

TIME DOESN'T HEAL TOXIC FAMILY WOUNDS

*We must be willing to let go of the life we planned
to have the life that is waiting for us.*
—JOSEPH CAMPBELL

My father always said he loved me, but his actions and words told a different story. For eighteen years, I lived in a domestically violent home where verbal, emotional, psychological, and spiritual abuse occurred daily. Instead of loving and nurturing me, my father constantly frightened me. His parenting style was a reign of terror.

I always felt love from my mom, but when it mattered most, she always stood by my dad. She excused, enabled, and defended his destructive and harmful behavior. All my hopes and dreams of a happy family, a loving childhood, and a thriving life were unrealized because of the anger, shame, guilt, and pain I experienced during my formative years.

How do you survive your toxic family and reclaim your life after toxic parents? I embarked on a three-year journey to answer

1

this vital question. I was desperate to find a solution to my family problems and heal the painful wounds from my past. Even after moving 1,200 miles away and spending many years estranged from my toxic family, my emotional scars remained.

Symptoms you may be suffering from toxic family wounds and trauma can include the following:

- Addiction
- Anger and rage
- Anxiety or panic attacks
- Codependency
- Conflict resolution difficulties
- Depression and hopelessness
- Difficulty concentrating and memory issues
- Eating disorders
- Feelings of numbness
- Fear
- Guilt
- Headaches
- Insomnia
- Irritability
- Isolation or avoiding relationships
- Loneliness
- Loss of control of emotions
- Nausea
- Numbing your pain with food, drugs, alcohol, or something else

- People-pleasing
- Post-traumatic stress (avoidance, flashbacks, persistent nightmares, recurring unwanted negative thoughts, intense emotional reactions to the present moment reminding you of your trauma)
- Problems at work
- Relationship problems
- Self-harm or suicidal ideation
- Stress
- Shame
- Trust issues

I experienced almost all the above symptoms because my family's toxicity was off the charts. Regardless of how many or how few of these symptoms you are experiencing, the principles and strategies in this book will help you survive your toxic family and reclaim your life.

The problem: Time does not heal toxic family wounds. Some life problems can be fixed over time, but toxic family wounds cannot. After walking away from the relationship with my father and after years of suffering, I realized I would never find true freedom until I dealt with the pain of my past.

The solution: Denying your pain or ignoring your past doesn't work. If it did, your past would already be healed and you wouldn't be reading this book. I don't know anyone who has successfully overcome their toxic family wounds by ignoring what happened to them. The good news is recovery is possible and doesn't need to be overly complicated.

No matter how toxic your family is or how much damage you've suffered, this book will help you begin your healing journey today. A multi-layered approach is necessary to overcome the adverse effects of your toxic family. The principles detailed in this book took me nearly a lifetime of mistakes to learn and three years to document and put into practice. Everything you are about to read comes from my personal experience. Through many years of trial and error, I learned that ignoring the pain and trauma of my past and hoping it would magically disappear on its own doesn't work. Even walking away and cutting ties with my family wasn't the solution I needed.

I promise if you follow these principles and strategies, your life will change dramatically! An amazing transformation will take place in you, and others will be drawn to your authenticity.

If you answer yes to any of the following questions, you will benefit from reading this book:

- Are you thinking about cutting ties and walking away from toxic family members?
- Do you feel like you are walking on eggshells and can't be yourself around certain family members?
- Is your family constantly picking fights with you?
- Do you feel unsettled or unsafe around your family?
- Do you suffer from negative thinking, overthinking, or a self-condemning inner critic because of your family?
- Does your family keep hurting you even after you tell them to stop?
- Are you living to please your family rather than living your authentic life?
- Are you afraid to pursue your dreams and follow your heart?
- Do you constantly feel that you are in trouble or that something is always wrong?

- Do you struggle with perfectionism to please your family?

- Does your family always try to change you or tell you what you should or should not do?

- Do you suffer from keeping secrets from your family?

- Are you soothing and self-medicating the pain your family has caused you with food, alcohol, drugs, or something else?

- Do you suffer from long-term anxiety and stress because of your family?

Throughout this book, you will find stress-relieving principles and strategies that will guide you step-by-step as you cope with the toxic family wounds that time won't heal. Your healing journey begins now if you are ready to take active steps to let go of your past and start living your authentic life today.

Let me briefly share my toxic family story: I was raised in a very religious home by an alcohol-abusing father full of violent rage and a loving mother who tolerated and enabled his destructive behavior. According to my mom, God was using the domestic violence and abuse we suffered to make us more like Jesus. I didn't need to attend seminary, which I eventually did, to realize this interpretation was utter nonsense.

Although I never confronted my father for fear that he would physically harm me, our relationship ended the day he kicked me out of the house at age eighteen. There was no turning back. After earning my BA in communications, I moved from Washington state to Los Angeles with some college friends. There I earned an MA in theology to untangle the religious mess my mother made of my spiritual life.

I rarely spoke to my father except to say, "Can you pass the phone to Mom?" My mom had a heart of gold, but years of domestic violence harmed her too. My dad was the source of our family's trauma. However, my mom became a co-conspirator when she enabled him and cited Bible verses to justify his destructive and harmful behavior.

Moving two states away didn't make my problems disappear, and time didn't heal my toxic family wounds. Despite my mistaken belief that leaving my family home would set me free, I found all my problems waiting for me in California, and my life went from bad to worse. I felt stuck in life and couldn't figure out how to get my parents off my back and out of my head.

Even though I was very successful in my career working at a major university in Southern California, I self-medicated almost every night with food and alcohol to numb my depression and post-traumatic stress. Unwanted negative thoughts filled my mind, and I overate and drank to soothe my pain and unhappiness. Eventually, I weighed 345 pounds, and my glass of wine at night spiraled into alcohol abuse. I was one order of chili-cheese fries away from a heart attack when my doctor told me I was morbidly obese, and my psychiatrist put me on anti-depressants which I took for nearly twenty years.

My true self remained hidden under many layers of toxic family scars and the masks I wore to protect myself. In my mind, I thought I was defective and unlovable, and so I became a people-pleaser, which was exhausting. Due to my toxic family trauma and secrets, I overate and abused alcohol for much of my life, resulting in obesity and dangerously high blood pressure. My life completely fell apart when I stopped taking anti-depressants in my late forties. After suffering a mental breakdown, I spent three years in and out of psychiatric hospitals.

After I recovered psychologically, three members of my immediate family passed away within three years. I began grieving those tragic deaths just as the Covid pandemic hit. This perfect storm of events caused me to wake up and take inventory of my life. My three-year journey to face the pain of my past started when I left my career and moved back to Washington state. I had to stop running from myself.

In addition to extensive therapy, I studied counseling, mindfulness, religion, and spirituality. I learned to journal and meditate. I became a crisis counselor and founded ToxicFamily. org to deepen my healing and help others in need. When I wasn't studying, counseling, or in therapy, I hiked the beautiful mountains and foothills of Washington's Olympic Peninsula. Eventually, I got down to a healthy weight and learned to drink responsibly by being present and practicing moderation and mindfulness.

During my recovery, I overcame addiction, anxiety, chronic depression, childhood trauma, codependency, fear, harassment, people-pleasing, post-traumatic stress, and toxic thinking. I broke free from the secrets that kept me a prisoner, and my spirituality thrived despite years of religious abuse. My anger, fear, guilt, and shame were replaced with love, joy, peace, and happiness. Though I am still a work in progress, I am finally living the authentic life I have been searching for since childhood.

In his novel *Talus*, Erol Ozan wrote, "Some beautiful paths can't be discovered without getting lost." Sometimes we feel lost when life is challenging us to take a new path, change our thinking, and swap out our old compass for a new one. Sometimes getting a little lost can wake you up and put you on the right path. Even though your family has let you down and life didn't turn out as you expected, it's never too late to discover your authentic self and life.

Now is the time to end your nightmare, follow your heart, trust your intuition, and fulfill your life and dreams. If you are reading this book, it means you are tired of suffering from family stress and anxiety. Stop thinking time will solve your toxic family problems, avoid the many mistakes I made, and start living your authentic life today!

The Toxic Family Solution is your compassionate guide and compass to help you find your way. Everything you need to know to survive your toxic family, take back your life, and realize your tremendous potential is awaiting your discovery.

Best wishes and peace on your healing journey,

STEVEN TODD BRYANT
FEBRUARY 14, 2023

CHAPTER 1

—⚜—

THE HARMFUL NATURE OF TOXIC FAMILIES

If it's destroying you, then it isn't love, my dear.

—UNKNOWN

The first step to surviving your toxic family and reclaiming your life after toxic parents is to identify the ways in which your toxic family harmed you.

This first chapter is about identifying the ways in which your family caused you pain and suffering. After reading this chapter, you will know for certain whether your family is toxic. Facing the harm and damage you experienced from your toxic family can be painful and overwhelming, but it is vital to your healing and recovery.

In this chapter, we will explore the following:

1. Journal Part I: Abandonment

2. Abuse Is Never Your Fault

3. How to Get Urgent Help

4. Identifying a Toxic Family

5. Wounds Caused by Toxic Families

6. Damage Caused by Secrets

7. Gaslighting

8. Roles that Hinder Self-Expression

9. Narcissists, Psychopaths & Sociopaths

Note: Each chapter begins with a short excerpt from my journal written during my recovery. Each chapter then provides tips for coping with your toxic family and principles for healing and recovery.

JOURNAL PART I: ABANDONMENT

Sometimes I wake up screaming. Screaming in a dream is called a *night terror*, a symptom of post-traumatic stress. Trauma is an emotional disturbance caused by a life-threatening or traumatizing event that causes physical or emotional harm. People who have experienced traumatic events, including abuse or domestic violence in toxic families, can experience night terrors. No matter how many years I spend in therapy, I can't seem to make the nightmares stop. I had another one just last week. I've been screaming in my dreams since I was a kid. Perhaps I need to start at the beginning.

When I was eight years old, my father woke me early one Saturday morning. He was about to show me how harmful a toxic family can be.

"Get up. We need to leave right now," he barked at me like a junkyard dog.

I don't remember showering or eating breakfast. Before I knew it, we were in our Volkswagen bus, a cargo van with no back seats. I sat on a World War II footlocker my dad had set up as a makeshift seat for me. The lack of seatbelts in the van seems unthinkable now. I always thought it was strange that my dad had bought a family car with only two seats, one for him and one for my mom. In my young mind, I believed it was a sign he didn't want me around. Later I would learn I was right.

Mom sat in the front passenger seat. I asked her, "Where are we going?"

"You'll see," she said quietly.

A few minutes later, my dad came to the VW carrying Ruby, the family cat. Ruby was a large black Siamese who followed me like my shadow. I loved her so much. Often, we would cuddle in the sun on our side porch. Ruby mostly lived inside, but we let her out occasionally. My dad handed her to me, and I could tell she was frightened, or maybe I was projecting my own fear.

"Why is Ruby coming with us?" I asked, because we never took Ruby anywhere in the car. Nobody responded. My mom and dad sat silently as my dad started up the VW. We didn't have a cat carrier, so I held her tightly in my arms and close to my heart. I was her seatbelt.

Dad drove us about a mile from our home in Seattle along the south end of Lake Washington. The sun was beginning to rise just as we passed the local tavern. After turning up a road, we entered a wooded area. Suddenly, Dad stopped the car and ordered me to open the door.

"Let Ruby out of the car. Do it now. Do it quickly, so you don't get caught."

"What?" I asked.

With angry black eyes, he yelled, "Do it!"

My dad made it clear by his tone that he meant business and questioning him today would have more severe consequences than usual. Living in my toxic family taught me how to read people. I didn't always know how I felt, but I could always sense the negative feelings in others.

I gently lowered Ruby's body to the ground, placing her on the gravel alongside the road. Tears filled my eyes.

"Don't you dare cry, mister," my father hissed. "Only girls and fags cry."

Under my breath, I said, "This is so screwed up!" I fought hard to stuff my emotions as usual.

"What did you say?" he growled.

"N-nothing," I stuttered in fear.

Dad turned forward, cranked the steering wheel hard, made a quick U-turn, and peeled out of the gravel, kicking up dust all over Ruby's face and body. I looked back and saw Ruby sitting on the side of the road, looking at me as if asking, "Why?"

As we drove away, I looked at both of my parents. Dad looked relieved, but Mom had a dazed look in her eyes.

Once we returned home, Dad went into the basement and began to cut wood with his large table saw he purchased on sale at Sears years earlier. He spent hours cutting wood in the basement but never created anything. I think his destruction of wood was his form of meditation. The dust and noise of the saw filled the house. I felt safe when he was in the basement because I knew where he was and I could breathe freely for just a minute or two. Mom was doing dishes and staring out the window.

"Mom, why did we leave Ruby in the woods?"

As she gently wiped my cheek where the tears had been, she said quietly, as if in a trance, "Ruby was pregnant."

Anger drowned out my sadness. I ran upstairs and slammed the door to my room. Mom ran behind me and whispered through the door, "Don't ever let your dad see your anger. Not ever."

In my room, I decided to hate my father from then on. Living with my family was nothing but a disappointment. I had to get out of there. I felt hopeless when I realized I was only eight and had ten more years to live in this hell-like prison. Soon after my dad forced me to abandon Ruby and her babies in the woods, I experienced my first night terror and started screaming in my dreams.

A few months later, we were on a day trip to my aunt and uncle's home in Olympia, Washington. My dad was in a bad mood, as usual. Dad got mad because of something my uncle had said and stormed out of their house. We quickly followed behind him, scrambling to get our day bags, coats, and Tupperware containers filled with the food we had brought but hadn't eaten.

Once in the car, my dad wasn't done. He turned his anger on my mom when she started having trouble reading the map. Dad yelled at Mom, ridiculing her for being "stupid" and unable to read "the damn map." Their fight escalated when Mom made a disrespectful comment to defend herself. Dad flipped out and started screaming at her. He slammed on the brakes and pulled the VW into a large hotel parking lot along the roadside.

"What the hell?" I said under my breath.

Like darts, my dad's angry black eyes stared back at me through the rearview mirror. I always tried to be the perfect son, but trying to be perfect never got me out of trouble. The familiar fear and terror I lived with every day possessed my whole being.

"What did you say?" he shouted.

"Nothing. I didn't say anything." I thought to myself, "Don't ever let him know what you are thinking. Don't ever let him know what you are feeling. Don't ever let him see your anger. Not ever."

"Get out of the car right now," he shouted.

"What? I didn't do anything wrong."

"Out of the car now," he demanded.

I knew he was serious, so I got out, and before I knew what was happening, they drove away.

Suddenly, I was standing alone in a parking lot one hundred miles from home. My parents had just abandoned me. In shock, I sat down on the curb. There was nobody to help me. I thought of how my father had told me a thousand times not to talk to strangers or discuss family problems with outsiders and to "always watch out for fags and perverts."

I remembered the story my dad told me about how his dad was a drunk and his parents abandoned him and placed him in an orphanage at age four. Dad always said they left him there because they didn't love him. As a child, I wondered why my father turned out to be just like his own dad, a drunk who abandoned his kids. I began to wonder if this was also my destiny.

Dad's practice of leaving family members on the side of the road had become a kind of family tradition. A year earlier, Dad got angry and left Mom and me on the side of the road in Bellevue, Washington. I was scared, but Mom took it in stride and said, "We are going to be OK. We just need to start walking home."

I saw her strength while we walked. She began sharing Bible verses she had memorized about how our suffering would make us more like Jesus. She said being left by Dad on the side of the road was a test of our faith, and Jesus would use it to make us stronger. I remember thinking to myself, "Uh, I don't think this is what Jesus had in mind."

This time was different because Mom wasn't there to help, and I couldn't think of any Bible verses. I sat on the curb and stared at my

14

Timex wristwatch my dad had given me for my birthday. Seconds seemed like hours. Many frightening thoughts went through my eight-year-old mind. Hating my dad made the situation seem more bearable. I said to myself, "I'll never let them hurt me again."

When my parents finally returned over an hour later, they didn't speak or apologize. Dad looked angry, and Mom stared straight ahead with a trance-like stare. I knew my relationship with them would never be the same. On the ride home, I began to count how many times my parents had broken my heart. I ran out of fingers and started counting toes. I remember thinking to myself, "So it's not just family pets who get left alone on the side of the road."

Although I didn't know it at the time, I would live in an abusive and domestically violent home for eighteen years. Nobody was ever physically injured, but much violence occurred. Nobody ever intervened. Nobody ever rescued me. The emotional, psychological, and spiritual damage was fierce and long-lasting.

THE HARMFUL NATURE OF YOUR TOXIC FAMILY

ABUSE IS NEVER YOUR FAULT

Your toxic family caused you to suffer, but it's not your fault. No matter how they treated you, it says nothing about who you are, your value as a person, or your true self. Your unhealthy family's behavior says everything about your family and nothing about you.

No matter how unhealthy your family is, you can overcome whatever happened to you! As soon as you accept the reality of the pain you have suffered, you will begin to feel a sense of freedom. Healing starts with facing the pain, trauma, and neglect you experienced from family members who were supposed to love, protect, and nurture you.

I was shocked when I learned all of the harmful effects of living in a toxic family. Almost every personal and relational problem I have ever experienced can be attributed to the abuse and domestic violence I suffered. As a child, I assumed all families were similar to mine and was unaware my family was domestically violent and abusive. I thought abuse was only sexual and domestic violence was only physical. But I was wrong.

There are seven types of domestic violence and abuse:

1. Emotional

2. Financial

3. Physical

4. Psychological

5. Sexual

6. Spiritual

7. Verbal

If you are being abused or live in a domestically violent home, you need to take immediate action to get help when it is safe to do so. Even if your abuser tells you, "You made me do this to you," abuse is never your fault. No matter what mistakes you might have made, abuse is never your fault. No matter what your family tells you, if you are in danger or in an unhealthy and unsafe situation, you must take care of yourself and get to a safe place as soon as possible.

HOW TO GET URGENT HELP

Abuse and domestic violence are very serious matters and should be addressed immediately. Get help now!

911

- If you are in immediate danger and are the victim of a serious crime, such as domestic violence, abuse, or sexual assault, get to a safe place and dial 911.

- 911 will dispatch emergency medical services, fire, and police.

- Available 24/7/365

988

- If you are experiencing a crisis, dial 988 for the Suicide & Crisis Lifeline or go to 988lifeline.org.

- You don't have to be suicidal to use 988. Anyone who is in crisis can reach out for help.

- 988 will provide suicide prevention and crisis counseling as well as information about available local resources.

- Available 24/7/365

NATIONAL DOMESTIC VIOLENCE HOTLINE

- thehotline.org
- Call, text, or chat 24/7/365
- The National Domestic Violence Hotline is a free twenty-four-hour confidential service for victims, survivors, and those affected by domestic violence, intimate partner violence, and relationship abuse.

LGBTQ+ HELP

TREVOR PROJECT: CRISIS COUNSELING & SUICIDE PREVENTION

- thetrevorproject.org

- Call, text, or chat 24/7/365

- Trevor Project is a free twenty-four-hour confidential service for LGBTQ+ crisis intervention & suicide prevention.

IDENTIFYING A TOXIC FAMILY

What is a toxic family? A toxic family is a dysfunctional family who does not respect the uniqueness of each family member, as evidenced by a lack of respect for personal boundaries. They blame, control, criticize, dismiss, punish, and threaten the people they are supposed to love. Their disrespect often escalates to abuse and domestic violence. Toxic family members enforce harmful rules and force family members to lie, keep secrets, and wear false masks instead of expressing their authentic selves. They judge your thoughts, deny your feelings, and destroy your dreams of a happy life. Substance abuse is also a common problem in toxic families, often manifested in excessive drinking and overeating.

No family member is immune from the damage caused by a toxic family. Rather than loving and caring for you, your family harmed and wounded you. Instead of preparing you for life, they damaged you by preventing you from achieving your maximum potential. They created an environment that robbed you of fully expressing your thoughts, feelings, and true identity.

CHARACTERISTICS OF A HEALTHY FAMILY

No family is perfect, and every family has some measure of dysfunction. To understand the extent of the damage your family caused you, let's first examine the characteristics of a healthy family. In a healthy family, everyone is loved, protected, nurtured, supported, and cared for, allowing them to express themselves in a safe and healthy manner. Social-emotional development is rooted in love, trust, and the freedom to safely express your authentic self.

Healthy families have the following attributes:

- Authentic self-expression is valued and nurtured, and individuality is encouraged.

- There is clear communication.

- There are consistent rules and rule enforcement.

- Emotional intelligence is practiced and taught.

- Emotional expression is valued and encouraged.

- There are healthy boundaries.

- Healthy conflict management and resolution are practiced.

- Honesty, trust, and mutual respect are modeled, taught, and valued.

- Mistakes are forgiven, and perfection is not expected or required.

- There is no abuse or domestic violence of any kind.

- There is no alcoholism or drug addiction.

- Food is not used as a coping mechanism.

- Outside relationships are encouraged.

- Parents lead by example.

- Problem-solving is accomplished through respectful communication.

- The physical, emotional, and spiritual health of each family member is nurtured.

- Physical punishment is non-abusive.

- There is respect for privacy and personal space.

- Survival skills to live a healthy life are modeled and taught.

- Teaching and training take place in a safe and supportive environment.

- Family members who are struggling with sexual orientation or gender identity issues are loved, guided, and helped with compassion and without homophobia or transphobia.

- There is unconditional love.

Through their words and actions, a healthy family conveys the following messages:

- You are OK, just as you are.

- You are enough.

- It's OK not to be perfect.

- You can overcome mistakes.

- You are accepted despite your weaknesses.

- You have the potential to overcome obstacles and achieve your dreams.

- You belong here.

- There's nothing wrong with you being you.

All of this is possible because a healthy family has unconditional love and trust as its foundation. Healthy family members stand on the shoulders of their healthy families to achieve their hopes, dreams, and aspirations. Healthy families do not shame or punish family members for being different or expressing their authentic selves. In a healthy family, being who you are is never wrong or a mistake.

Nobody is perfect. Perfection is impossible. Healthy families accept the authentic uniqueness of family members and nurture them without trying to alter or change their essential nature.

CHARACTERISTICS OF AN UNHEALTHY FAMILY

The following are typical characteristics of unhealthy families:

- There is abuse and domestic violence (emotional, financial, physical, psychological, sexual, spiritual, verbal).
- There is alcoholism or drug addiction.
- Authentic self-expression is judged, viewed negatively, and discouraged ("What's wrong with you?").
- Communication is unclear, one way, and closed (top-down communication, parent gives orders, lack of dialogue).
- Emotional expression is not valued and encouraged; primary emotions are sad, happy, afraid, and angry.
- Emotional intelligence is not encouraged.
- Food is used as a drug or coping mechanism.
- Honesty, trust, and mutual respect are not modeled, taught, and valued.
- Inconsistent rules and rule enforcement.
- Love is conditional.
- Mistakes are not forgiven, and perfection is expected and required.
- Outside relationships are discouraged.
- Parents do not lead by example.
- Problem-solving or problem-resolution skills are lacking.

- The physical, emotional, and spiritual health of each family member are not nurtured.

- Physical punishment is abusive and violent.

- Respect for privacy and personal space is lacking.

- Sexual orientation or gender identity must be heterosexual and gender normative (homophobia, transphobia, heterosexism).

- Survival skills to live a healthy life are not modeled or taught.

- Teaching and training do not take place. (Parent assumes child already knows how to do everything.)

- There are unhealthy boundaries.

- There is unhealthy conflict management and resolution.

Having an unhealthy family discourages the development of who you are, forcing you to guard your heart, question your intuition, and abandon your dreams. Essentially, they ask you to betray and abandon your true self. Conditional love, nonacceptance, and unhealthy boundaries characterize relationships in toxic families.

Toxic families fail to teach you that you are perfectly OK just as you are, negatively affecting your identity, self-esteem, and self-worth. Toxic families punish you for making mistakes and discourage you from expressing your true nature. To survive, you must lie about yourself and others, follow their rules, and suppress your intellectual, emotional, and self-expression.

Even if your family told you they loved you a thousand times and you can remember loving moments you shared with your toxic family, the number of times they hurt you tells the whole story. Displays of love and affection combined with mistreatment and abuse are damaging, confusing, and crazy making. Despite the sincerity of their love, their good intentions do not justify the harm they caused you. Maya Angelou said, "When someone shows you who they are, believe them the first time." The first time your toxic family harmed you, they showed you who they were. Believe them!

WOUNDS CAUSED BY TOXIC FAMILIES

When you realize how much harm your toxic family has caused you, it can be overwhelming. Although each family is different, and toxicity levels vary, the following potential wounds may occur in toxic families:

- Abandonment or fear of abandonment
- Abuse and domestic violence
- Addiction, alcoholism, drug abuse
- Anxiety and stress
- Parentification, where child is put into a parental role (where a child is made to be a confidant, sounding board, or caretaker or assume parental duties such as cooking all the meals or being responsible for things a parent would normally do)
- Cognitive distortions or thinking errors such as all-or-nothing thinking, catastrophizing, or personalization
- Codependency (an unhealthy dependence on another person)
- Eating disorders (undereating, overeating, anorexia, bulimia, obesity, unconscious eating)
- Failed external relationships, poor or no relationships outside of the family; a high level of alertness in maintaining external relationships, which is emotionally exhausting

- False sense of reality caused by keeping family secrets and being forced to lie about who you are and how you are feeling
- Fear of being punished just for being yourself
- Feelings of inadequacy
- Fragile sense of self
- Gaslighting (manipulating another person by causing them to question their interpretation of reality)
- Hypersensitivity to invalidation and a constant need for validation
- Humor as a veiled threat or at the expense of others
- Insecurity
- Insomnia
- Isolating
- Job instability
- Lack of authentic identity formation and development
- Lack of emotional intelligence (feelings are limited to sad, happy, afraid, and angry)
- Lack of self-awareness (tendency to blame the outside world for your problems)
- Lack of self-care (self-neglect)
- Lack of self-esteem and self-worth; not valuing yourself, not loving yourself, hating or loathing yourself; lacking self-confidence, self-trust, feeling unlovable or unworthy of love
- Inability to be your authentic self because it feels unsafe (lying to yourself and others)

- Nagging feelings of guilt (you are always in trouble), shame (something is wrong with you), self-blame (what goes wrong is always your fault)
- Obsessive-compulsive behaviors (avoidance, arranging, checking, counting, isolation, obsessive thoughts)
- Overly self-conscious
- Overthinking and overanalyzing
- Perfectionism (inner self-criticism and the need to be perfect, which mimics your parents' criticism of you)
- Privacy disrespected or ignored
- Prone to hopelessness (belief there is no hope of improving your situation), helplessness (belief there is no action you can take to improve your situation), and depression (low mood with sadness and decreased interest in life activities)
- Prone to repeat dysfunctional relationships patterns learned in the unhealthy family setting in relationships external to the family
- Prone to substance abuse and self-medication to cope with the pain of past traumatic and negative experiences (alcohol, drugs, food, sex)
- Prone to anxiety, fear, stress, and worry
- Rigid, dogmatic, judgmental, and unaccepting approach to self, others, life, religion
- Self-harm
- Sexual orientation and gender identity issues (homophobia, transphobia, heterosexism)
- Shame, a form of self-hatred
- "Should" and "should not" statements

- Suicidal ideation

- Tendency to isolate (avoiding social situations due to feelings of anxiety, depression, shame, or guilt) to avoid further pain (it's easier to be alone or limit relationships)

- Trust issues

- Unhealthy boundaries (either between family members or with outsiders, the words "no" and "stop" mean nothing)

- Use of religion or Bible verses to shame, manipulate, control, or justify abuse and mistreatment

- Control or restriction of access to money

- Symptoms of post-traumatic stress (PTSD):

  o Avoidance, flashbacks, persistent upsetting nightmares and night terrors, recurring unwanted negative thoughts, and intense emotional reactions to the present moment reminding you of your trauma

My family was highly toxic, and I experienced almost all the above adverse effects. Your personal experience will be different. Regardless of how many or how few of these wounds you experienced, the principles and strategies found in this book will help you move forward toward healing. If you feel overwhelmed by your toxic family wounds or need one-on-one support, chapter 5 discusses long-term solutions for getting help.

DAMAGE CAUSED BY SECRETS

Toxic families are full of secrets. People keep all kinds of secrets to survive their unhealthy families. Family members keep secrets for various reasons, but the most common reasons are to avoid pain, humiliation, or punishment. Your family may have kept secrets from each other as well as from people outside the family. Additionally, there may be secrets known only to a few family members or even one member, such as extramarital affairs, financial difficulties, gambling or drug addictions, or issues related to sexual identity and gender non-conformity.

My father regularly warned me never to tell anyone outside of the family about the abuse and domestic violence taking place within our family. For years, I kept secrets to survive in my toxic family, which caused me tremendous fear, guilt, shame, pain, and suffering. I can tell you from personal experience the consequences of keeping secrets for years can be devastating. When you keep a secret, you are basically lying to others about some aspect of who you are. Keeping a secret can be frightening and shameful if you live in a family where they punish liars or are negative, condemning, and judgmental.

You can suffer long-term adverse effects from keeping secrets, whether they are your own or those of your loved ones. When you share your secrets with safe, supportive, and empathetic people, they begin to lose their power over you, helping you overcome loneliness, fear, and shame.

The damaging effects of keeping family secrets can include the following:

- Alcohol and drug abuse
- Anxiety
- Backaches
- Digestive problems
- Guilt
- Headaches
- Insecurity

- Isolation

- Lack of well-being

- Low self-esteem

- Obesity

- Self-doubt

- Shame

- Trust issues

- Resentment

- Stress

The first time you share your secrets may be frightening, but you will experience great freedom and relief when you become honest about every aspect of yourself. To reclaim your life, you must find someone with whom you can safely share your secrets. While living in a toxic home, sharing your secrets with your family may not be safe, but I encourage you to find a trusted person outside the family to help you carry your burden as soon as possible. Until you are ready to share your secrets with others, you can write about them in a journal (see chapter 5).

GASLIGHTING

Gaslighting is a form of abuse toxic family members use to control and manipulate their loved ones. Gaslighting occurs when the parent or family member tries to cause the victim to question their sanity, perception of reality, or memories of what happened. The term originated from a 1944 film called *Gaslight*, where a husband tried to convince his wife she imagined things to drive her insane and control her behavior. Gaslighters will create a false narrative to shift the blame for what happened from themselves onto someone or something else. In some cases, gaslighters attempt to convince their victims that what they remember never happened or the abuse they experienced was not as severe as they recall.

The following are examples of gaslighting statements:

- "Can't you take a joke?"
- "Don't be so dramatic."
- "I'm sorry you think that's what happened."
- "I never did/said that."
- "It didn't happen like that."
- "It didn't really hurt."
- "That's not what happened."
- "You're crazy."
- "You're just imagining things."
- "You're overreacting."
- "You're making a big deal over nothing."
- "You're remembering it wrong."
- "You're too sensitive."
- "You're totally misinterpreting what is happening."

Gaslighting is prevalent in toxic families. Every time I tried to raise concerns with my parents about problems within the family, gaslighting was their go-to response. Gaslighting causes the victim to doubt themselves and question their interpretation of reality and makes them feel defective and deficient in their ability to judge and interpret what is happening around them. Gaslighting can cause anxiety and depression, suppress the development of the authentic self, and contribute to psychological trauma. If you suspect a family member is gaslighting you, you can always ask a friend or therapist for a second opinion. If someone refuses to stop gaslighting you after you confront them, you must either walk away from the relationship or keep them at a safe distance.

ROLES THAT HINDER SELF-EXPRESSION

Family members in dysfunctional homes learn to play roles they choose or are assigned. Your toxic family prevented you from being yourself, forcing you to wear false masks and play dysfunctional roles to survive. Playing a role and hiding who you are to survive in a toxic family prevented you from developing and expressing your true identity and authentic self. You and your significant relationships outside your family will suffer if you are unaware of these destructive roles and don't act to become your authentic self in all current relationships.

The following are examples of roles family members play in a toxic family:

- Clown
- Confidant
- Enabler
- Golden child
- Scapegoat
- Substance abuser

CLOWN

Clowns use humor to lighten the family's negative and dysfunctional mood when family life becomes too intense. Clowns believe they can prevent abuse or violence by keeping the family laughing and distracted. The clown will always be on high alert and ready at any moment to elevate the family's mood. Clowns constantly look for changes in the family's emotional state and behavior and thus lose connection with their own emotional condition. Clowns develop a reverse emotional intelligence, where they become highly sensitive and attuned to other people's emotions but not their own. Throughout their lives, clowns will likely be anxious, on alert, and hypersensitive to changes in mood and behavior in all relationships. The clown seeks to help the family at the expense of their own emotional development.

CONFIDANT

Confidants are children who unhealthy parents entrust with their secrets. A parent may use their child as a sounding board, best friend, informal therapist, or a source of advice and support. This role forces the child to provide emotional support, advise the parent, and become the parent's emotional caregiver. Because the child lacks the emotional maturity needed to handle adult issues, they are forced to take on the role of the adult in the relationship, called *parentification*. This role reversal damages the child's long-term emotional well-being and is a subtle form of child abuse. Any child who becomes a confidant or feels they need to protect their parent from harm will suffer emotional damage. Confidants learn to ignore their own feelings and neglect their own needs. As adults, they may develop long-term problems such as anxiety, depression, substance abuse, or eating disorders.

ENABLER

The enabler helps dysfunctional family members perpetuate and continue harmful and unhealthy behaviors. They may even adopt the same addictive and destructive behaviors to avoid conflict with addicted family members. For example, a wife of an alcoholic may become a heavy drinker to enable and please her spouse. Often in denial, the enabler will overlook the destructive and harmful behavior of the unhealthy family member as well as the harm they are doing to the family. Despite offering a nurturing aspect to the family, enablers can inhibit the ability of the family to resolve problems, heal, or seek help. Enablers frequently repeat this role in relationships outside the family and are often attracted to relationships where they can help or fix others.

GOLDEN CHILD

The golden child is the family's favorite, the chosen one, the child who can do no wrong. Families treat the golden child as special and gifted. The family celebrates the golden child for their achievements, usually at school or in the community, and overlooks their weaknesses and faults. The golden child feels intense pressure to keep the family together and avoids making mistakes for the good of the family. Even though perfection is unattainable, the golden child often struggles with perfectionism. Everyone has faults, and no one is perfect. Maintaining a healthy relationship requires accepting the weaknesses and failings of yourself and others.

SCAPEGOAT

In dysfunctional families, scapegoats are the opposite of the golden child. The family blames the scapegoat for all their troubles and bad luck, believing this person is the source of all family problems. The scapegoat serves to distract attention from the real problem, which is the unhealthy family itself. A scapegoat may be the only member of the family who rebels or speaks out, because they believe they have nothing to lose.

SUBSTANCE ABUSER

In many cases, the family's substance abuser is also the head of the family. The substance abuser may also be a child or spouse who adopts addictive behaviors to cope with and soothe the pain of the dysfunctional family. Substance abuse can include alcohol, drugs, food, or any substance used to relieve pain, soothe, and self-medicate. Substance abuse and obesity in dysfunctional families are often multi-generational. Addictions persist from generation to generation, despite causing severe health consequences and sometimes death. Those who grew up with a substance abuser may also exhibit similar behaviors, even if they are not addicted themselves. A spouse or child of an alcoholic may also experience symptoms like addiction, including anxiety, mood swings, and depression. If you or a family member is a substance abuser, get help. (See chapter 2.)

NARCISSISTS, PSYCHOPATHS & SOCIOPATHS

The following are dangerous roles found in some unhealthy families:

- Narcissist
- Psychopath
- Sociopath

NARCISSIST

Narcissists have an unhealthy and exaggerated sense of self-importance and believe they deserve special privileges and treatment because they are more intelligent and gifted than everyone else. Narcissists need others to admire them. They dominate discussions, have relationship difficulties, and manipulate people

33

and circumstances. Narcissists do not consider how their actions impact others, lack empathy, and are inconsiderate of the feelings of others. Deep down, the narcissist is highly sensitive to criticism and has feelings of shame, insecurity, and vulnerability which may be unconscious. Those who live with narcissists over an extended period may experience low self-esteem, question their self-worth, and experience anxiety, depression, and post-traumatic stress.

Setting boundaries is essential when you are in a relationship with a narcissist. (See chapter 4). A boundary statement may be as simple as, "It's not OK for you to talk to me that way," or, "It's not OK for you to treat me that way." Narcissists may be frustrated by the boundaries you put in place, causing them to erupt in anger. Whenever a narcissist fails to respect your limits, you must decide whether to remain in the relationship or cut ties and walk away.

PSYCHOPATH/SOCIOPATH (ANTISOCIAL PERSONALITY DISORDER)

People with antisocial personality disorders (APSD) are also known as psychopaths and sociopaths. Because they are pathologically prone to domestically violent behavior without remorse or guilt, they are the most harmful members of a toxic family. While the chances of having someone with APSD in your family are low, you must be aware of their dangerous behavior.

Characteristics of those with antisocial personality disorders may include the following:

- Few long-term relationships
- Impulsive behavior and failure to meet job and family responsibilities
- Lack of concern about the safety of self or others

- Lack of remorse, guilt, or empathy
- Unable to control feelings of anger

If you believe you are in a relationship with someone with an antisocial personality disorder, seek help from a professional as soon as possible.

CHAPTER ONE SUMMARY

The first step to surviving your toxic family & reclaiming your life after toxic parents is to identify the ways in which your toxic family harmed you. In this chapter, we explored how abuse is never your fault, how to get urgent help, and how to identify a toxic family. We discussed the wounds caused by toxic families, damage caused by secrets, gaslighting, roles that hinder self-expression, and narcissists, psychopaths, and sociopaths. In chapter 2, we will explore how to cope with your toxic family.

CHAPTER 2

COPING WITH YOUR TOXIC FAMILY

Life is not the way it's supposed to be, it's the way it is.
The way you cope with it is what makes the difference.
—VIRGINIA SATIR

**The second step to surviving your toxic family and
reclaiming your life after toxic parents is to learn
healthy coping behaviors and strategies.**

Thinking about your toxic family and their harmful behavior is stressful, but there is freedom in learning ways to overcome their dysfunction. This chapter will focus on how to be healthy around unhealthy family members. By trial and error, you may have already learned some strategies that work for you, and after reading this chapter, you'll be an expert.

In this chapter, we will explore the following:

1. Journal Part II: Unsafe

2. Strategies for Spending Time with Unhealthy Families

3. Healthy Coping Behaviors

4. Unhealthy Coping Behaviors

5. Substance Abuse, Excessive Drinking & Overeating

6. Coping with Negative Emotions

JOURNAL PART II: UNSAFE

Saturday night was often spaghetti night in our house. Our family always looked forward to Mom's famous spaghetti. Dad would even participate in the fun by adding his special seasoning of wine and beer to the spaghetti sauce. Mom's spaghetti was served cafeteria style, with the sauce mixed in with the noodles. Typically, we ate in the dining room, but on spaghetti night, we always ate in the kitchen.

Despite my father's rage, abuse, and domestic violence, my mom always tried hard to make our house fun and seem ordinary. She worked extra hard in the kitchen to add some normalcy to our lives. She tried to make holidays joyful and festive, decorating the house with seasonal flair. Sadly, if my father didn't cancel holidays or special occasions at the last minute, I could always count on him to ruin them with drunken episodes or angry outbursts.

I'll never forget the Saturday evening I ran into the kitchen eagerly anticipating gobs of spaghetti and French bread. There was nothing unusual about this Saturday night until I noticed our spaghetti dinner was splattered on the kitchen wall, half stuck and half sliding down as if in slow motion. A family heirloom plate, once beloved by my mother, lay shattered in a thousand pieces on the floor next to the kitchen table, covered with spaghetti sauce and noodles.

My parent's fight had stopped, but tensions were high. Dad was furious, and my mom was afraid. In shock and disbelief, I kept looking back and forth at my parents and the spaghetti dinner on the wall and the floor. I didn't know what had happened, but I knew how to feel—afraid. I figured Mom must have said something that triggered my dad's anger, causing him to throw our dinner at the wall. Or maybe Mom threw the dinner at the wall in an act of defiance and independence. Nobody ever said a word about what happened, so I'll never know.

Mom placed fresh plates of spaghetti in front of us a few moments later and tried to pretend everything was normal again. She always made a huge vat of spaghetti, so the vast quantity sprayed on the wall was only a tiny portion of what she had prepared. Trying to eat spaghetti with broken dishes at my feet and food on the walls and floor made me sick to my stomach. I pushed the spaghetti around on my plate, trying not to stare at my angry parents in this bizarre scene. Everyone pretended nothing had happened.

Playing the role of the clown and trying to get my family back to normal, I hummed a song I had heard on a TV advertisement the night before. I always played the role of the clown in our family and tried to ensure everyone else was OK despite how I felt. I wasn't very in touch with my emotions, but I always knew how everybody else felt. I had four primary feelings: sad, happy, afraid, and angry. I didn't like to be angry because my dad had enough rage for the whole family.

Dad snapped at me angrily, "No singing at the table!" Dad always imposed new family rules at the dinner table. He had already outlawed almost every possible topic of conversation at dinnertime, so we spent most dinners staring out the window in silence. After dinner, Dad refilled his drink and moved to his recliner in front of the TV. He either drank beer or whiskey or sometimes both until he fell asleep. That night was a beer and whiskey night. I went to bed around 8:00 p.m. to spend less time with my father, and because the tension was so thick, you could cut it with a knife.

"Night, Mom." I kissed her on the cheek.

"Good night, honey." Mom kissed me back.

"Good night," I said tenuously to my dad.

He replied, "Don't make too much noise up in your room. We can hear everything you do up there."

"OK, love you too," I said, still stunned by all that had happened.

Once in bed, I noticed Dad turned up the TV so loud I could hear it up the stairs, down the hall, and on the other side of the house. I always wondered if he turned up the TV just to keep me awake or if he didn't realize how his actions affected others. Maybe he just didn't care anymore. Most fathers find meaning in life by providing for and protecting their families. My dad had lost his way in life a long time ago and resented the role of father he had to play.

Eventually, I drifted off to sleep. Being raised in an abusive family made me a light sleeper, a problem I still have to this day. It's hard to sleep with one ear open. Cats do it all the time, but not humans. The fear of my dad's violent rage caused me to feel unsafe all the time. I was in a deep sleep when the yelling started again.

"What the hell is wrong with you?" Dad yelled with condescension toward Mom.

I checked the clock, and it was just past midnight. The neighbors had to be hearing this violent outburst. As my father raged, his voice increased in volume. He was a large man, and I feared for mom's safety as well as my own. Hearing my mother yell back at him in self-defense was always a frightening experience. "Don't pick a fight with him," I would think to myself. I felt sorry for her and afraid for her at the same time. He terrified me. Pulling my blanket over my head, I tried to make my family disappear.

I felt terror because I knew when he was finished with my mom, I could be his next victim. After verbally abusing my mom, he often marched up the creaky stairs, stomped down the long hallway to my bedroom, threw open my bedroom door, and verbally abused and bullied me. My heart pounded whenever I heard the creaking sounds of his large footsteps.

Mom never spoke up when dad went off on me. She probably thought his abuse would help build my character, or maybe she just felt powerless to do anything. I always wondered why a grown man would terrify a little kid. I could never figure out why my dad was so angry, but I always feared his rage would turn to physical violence, putting our lives in danger or worse. That night I was lucky. Mom took the brunt of his temper, and he must have fallen asleep again in his chair. I spent the rest of the night awake. Dad taught me to be vigilant. Now I call it post-traumatic stress.

I was always puzzled why my mom stayed with my dad. I always figured she stayed because she was madly in love with him. I couldn't see or make sense of it. Love is strange. Some moms love their husbands more than their kids. Other moms love their kids more than their husbands. Mom always put Dad first, and she loved me the best she could, given the circumstances. When Mom and I were alone together, I felt the full and undistracted power of her motherly love, and it was amazing.

Even though it doesn't make any sense, I always blamed myself for everything that went wrong in my family. I always figured I had done something wrong. Kids often blame themselves for things they can't understand or control. Despite my best efforts to be the perfect child, I constantly feared I was to blame for all my parent's problems. My solution was to try to be perfect. The big problem was my father's expectations, and requirements were constantly shifting, making being perfect a moving target. What pleased him yesterday didn't always work today. Trying to be perfect will mess with your mind. Trust me, I know.

No matter what I did or didn't do, I could never be the perfect son, and he constantly shamed me for not meeting his expectations.

41

Instead of saying, "Let's talk about the mistake you made," he would say, "What's wrong with you?" I always felt defective and like being myself was wrong. I got in trouble just for being me. My dad always believed he was right and he knew best, and if you didn't see things his way, something was wrong with you.

Just about the time I turned nine, the only thing I feared more than my father's violence was his discovering I was gay. I could only imagine what nightmare awaited me if he discovered my secret. Because of my dad's rage and my mom's judgmental and unaccepting version of religion, I had to hide my sexuality from everyone. Finding out I was gay at such an early age was probably the worst thing that could have happened to me, on top of the daily terror and abuse I was already experiencing. My dad daily made homophobic comments and regularly displayed his fear and hatred of homosexuals. Most parents say, "I love you," when you leave the house. Every day when I left for school, my dad warned me to "watch out for all the fags and perverts." So many times, I thought to myself, "But what if I am one?"

I always believed no matter how many times my dad verbally abused me, the day he found out I was gay would be the day his abuse would turn to physical violence. My mom believed all homosexuals went to Hell, even if they asked Jesus to forgive them of their sins. Apart from being theologically incorrect, this belief messed me up big time.

The morning after the spaghetti incident, my dad warned, "You better not tell anyone at school about the spaghetti fight last night. Remember, we're a happy family. Don't ever tell strangers our family secrets. Don't tell anyone at school what happens in this family."

I always had great relationships with my teachers. Upon arriving at school, my favorite teacher hugged me and asked, "Did you have a good evening last night?" I wanted to say, "I think I'm gay, my father is abusing me, and I feel unsafe in my house." Instead, I lied to protect my father for fear of the negative consequences of being myself and telling the truth. I felt dirty telling lies to those who cared about me.

My parents always ensured I had clothes to wear, food to eat, and a roof over my head. They took me to the doctor and dentist and paid for braces to straighten my teeth. They always made sure I went to school and received a good education. But they failed to provide me with the psychological and emotional well-being a healthy child needs to develop into a healthy adult. My authentic self was buried beneath my toxic family wounds. My parents taught me how to lie about myself and the hell we lived in.

COPING WITH YOUR TOXIC FAMILY

STRATEGIES FOR SPENDING TIME WITH UNHEALTHY FAMILIES

Toxic family members can make you feel angry, fearful, and stressed out. Any time you spend with your toxic family can drain the life out of you. Thankfully, there are strategies you can use to make spending time with toxic family members less stressful. Using the following techniques, you can minimize anxiety and add inner calm to your interactions with your toxic family. Always remember your health and well-being must be your top priority, especially in an unhealthy environment.

Below are healthy strategies you can use when spending time with your unhealthy family:

- Always breathe, be present, and be aware of your body. Stay mindful of your negative thoughts and remain in the moment. Remain grounded when your family loses touch with reality. Don't get stuck in your head. Feel your fingers, feet, and toes to remind yourself you have a body.

- Avoid negative thinking and cognitive errors such as all-or-nothing thinking, catastrophizing, or personalization. (See chapter 6.)

- Be cautious of anyone in your family who frequently tells you what you "should" or "should not" do. They may be trying to control, manipulate, or change you. Avoid spending too much time around people who don't accept you and want to change you.

- Do not ask unhealthy family members for advice, and be careful when they offer it (which they constantly do). If they do not accept you just as you are, their advice will always be about changing you to be like them or to become the person they want you to be. Manipulative and controlling family members will offer advice whether you ask for it or not, often using "should" or "should not" statements. When unhealthy family members offer unsolicited advice, say, "Thank you, I'll keep that in mind," or, "I'll think about that," or, "I don't agree, but let's agree to disagree."

- Be organic with your words and thoughts. Don't waste time on the car ride to your family home preparing the words you might say if they say something offensive or hurtful. Be in the moment. It is better to be present and organic, dealing with life as it happens and speaking honestly from your heart than reciting a pre-prepared speech. Worrying about the future is an energy drain.

- Before and after family visits, take a social media break from unhealthy family members if needed.

- Change the subject or make a joke if the conversation gets too serious or heavy.

- Don't argue viewpoints, and always allow others to have differing opinions. You don't have to be right all the time or have everyone always agree with you. Your value and worth as a human being have nothing to do with your point of view.

- Don't ever base your value or worth on the opinions of others.

- Don't be surprised when people with a history of losing their temper get upset.

- Don't change your behavior to please others. Always be your authentic self, and never be ashamed of who you are. You are never wrong for being yourself. Being you is never a mistake. If you can't be yourself around someone, spend limited time around them.

- Don't engage when abusive and bullying family members pick a fight. Let it go. Their only goal is to humiliate or control you. Don't take the bait or react to something said to upset you, destabilize you, or make you lose your temper.

- Don't slip into the dysfunctional roles detailed in the last chapter (clown, confidant, enabler, golden child, scapegoat, or substance abuser).

- Don't try to shame your family the way they shamed you. Don't try to hurt your family the way they hurt you. Always take the high road.

- Don't take responsibility for what you cannot control, which is a lot.

- Don't take their behavior personally. It's never about you.

- Don't try to be perfect or expect others to be perfect. Nobody has ever accomplished this. Every human is flawed. Allow for human weakness and mistakes in yourself and your relationships.

- Don't try to change or fix your family. People will only change when they are ready to change.

- Leave if you must. You don't need to leave mad or give an explanation.

- Love your unhealthy family members from a safe distance. Tell your family you are unavailable this year for special events if you need to stay away to protect yourself.

- Never feel obligated to share private information with an unhealthy family member. Never share your heart with people who have already shown you they don't accept you as you are and want to change you.

- Reduce the length and frequency of your family visits.

- Set boundaries, and don't be surprised if unhealthy family members get angry when you assert yourself. "No!" is a complete sentence. "I don't want to talk about that right now!" is a perfectly healthy response. (See chapter 4 for more on boundaries.)

- Take a walk outside when you need some fresh air and perspective. Take a break when you need one. To find calm, go to the bathroom to collect your thoughts or clear your mind.

- Use cocktail party rules: (1) Avoid talking about yourself: Ask others, "So what's new with you?" (2) Keep the conversation light and avoid deep questions. (3) Don't discuss religion, politics, health, diet, or other hot topics you know will upset them and trigger conflict or unhealthy behavior.

- Repeat positive self-affirmations such as "I am enough!" "I am OK, just as I am!" and, "I can be OK even if others are not OK."

- Try not to let your visit cause you to feel hopeless or depressed. Stay in the moment and do not project negative thoughts and feelings about your family and yourself into the future.

- After you visit your family, reach out to a safe, supportive, and empathetic person to destress and debrief. Consider journaling your experience and meditating or praying if necessary.

- See your therapist before and after your family visit if needed.

Pick one or two of the above strategies every time you spend time with your family. Find the ones that work best for you, and if you are in therapy, share your successes and failures with your therapist. When spending time with your toxic family, express your authentic self and protect your well-being at all times. You must take action when your family tries to control, manipulate, shame, humiliate, or change you. If necessary, you can always leave.

HEALTHY COPING BEHAVIORS

A coping behavior is a method of dealing with the stress and pain of your toxic family. There are both healthy and unhealthy coping behaviors. Your parents likely taught you a combination of healthy and unhealthy coping behaviors, which you find yourself repeating when life gets stressful. Your challenge is to make healthy coping choices when facing stressful thoughts about yourself, life, and how others treat you. Rather than making unhealthy coping choices, you can manage your stress with healthy coping behaviors that benefit you rather than harm you.

Healthy coping behaviors may not resolve the underlying issues causing your pain, but they will help you cope with stress by not adding to your problems or harming your health. The following healthy coping behaviors may assist you in alleviating the pain you may be experiencing around your toxic family:

- Be grateful. (Consciously look for things to be thankful for.)
- Be mindful by accepting yourself, others, and life without judgment. (Mindfulness and acceptance never mean staying in abusive situations.)
- Find a distraction. (This is not avoidance, but doing something different to take a momentary break from the difficult situation.)
- Exercise to relieve stress.
- Focus on the positive. (Watch negative thinking.)
- Focus on your breathing.
- Journal.
- Meditate.
- Pray or practice spirituality.
- Talk with safe and supportive friends and family.
- Talk to your therapist.
- Turn your pain into something to help others. (Write a book, teach a class, write a blog.)

Healthy coping behaviors can help you remain present while dealing with toxic family members and identify any negative emotions you may be experiencing. For more healthy coping behaviors, see chapter 5, "Examples of Self-Care Activities."

UNHEALTHY COPING BEHAVIORS

Below are some examples of unhealthy coping behaviors your parents may have modeled for you:

- Avoidance (avoiding the issue causing stress)
- Drug use
- Eating disorders (undereating, overeating, anorexia, bulimia, obesity, unconscious eating)
- Engaging in risky behaviors
- Escapism
- Excessive alcohol use
- Gambling
- Ignoring feelings
- Impulsive spending
- Isolation and withdrawal from others
- Not taking care of yourself (lack of hygiene)
- Overworking
- Refusing help from others
- Sabotaging self or others
- Self-harm
- Sex (excessive masturbation and promiscuity to fill the emotional void of wanting to be loved)

- Sleeping too much or too little

- Smoking

- Toxic thinking and cognitive errors such as all-or-nothing thinking, catastrophizing & personalization

- Unhealthy expressions of anger that harm others and you

To survive your toxic family and regain your life, you must identify what underlying issues are causing your pain. Talking about your harmful family experience with a therapist or a trusted friend can help you gain perspective and insight into why you are using unhealthy coping behaviors to manage your pain. Instead of unhealthy coping behaviors, find healthy ones that reduce your anxiety and stress without harming you.

SUBSTANCE ABUSE, EXCESSIVE DRINKING & OVEREATING

To deal with the stress of their toxic families, many people turn to substance abuse, excessive alcohol use, or overeating to cope with their emotional and psychological pain. Excessive drinking and overeating are often passed down from generation to generation. If you struggle with either, there's a good chance your parents did too. On top of the toxic family issues you already have, excessive drinking and overeating can lead to new health problems, such as high blood pressure, heart problems, sleep apnea, liver disease, and digestive issues.

I remember as a child, saying, "I will never be like my father. I will be the exact opposite of my father in every way." And yet, as an adult, I mimicked his drinking and overeating to overcome stress and anxiety since I did not know any other ways to cope. As a result of my obesity and alcohol abuse, I suffered many of the same health problems as my father.

Rather than using alcohol or food to numb and soothe your pain, it is always better to face your pain directly. When you are suffering from overeating or alcohol abuse, or any other type of addiction or substance abuse, you need to reduce the effects of your harmful behavior as quickly as possible. When you abuse substances to manage your pain, the substance has the potential to take control of your life.

Important note: Consult your physician before changing your diet or stopping or reducing your alcohol or drug consumption. Without your doctor's supervision, changing your diet or withdrawing from drugs or alcohol may trigger life-threatening health complications.

STOP DRINKING ALCOHOL COMPLETELY

If you decide you want to stop drinking alcohol completely, Alcoholics Anonymous (AA) aa.org has a long track record of successfully helping people overcome alcohol abuse through abstinence.

BE CONSCIOUS OF YOUR ACTIONS

Learn to be present whenever you eat food or drink alcohol. Be careful when you eat or drink while performing other activities, like surfing the web or watching television. One way to be present is to focus on what the alcohol is doing to your body. When eating, pay attention to your stomach and stop when it is full, if not before. Despite what your parents might have told you, you don't have to eat everything on your plate. Unconsciously eating or drinking is a recipe for trouble. Be aware of how many times you fill your glass and how many times you get another helping of food. To practice moderation, you must not be in denial, distracted, or worrying about the past or the future. To gain control over any substance abuse, you need to be living in the present moment and conscious of your behavior.

GET HELP FOR SUBSTANCE ABUSE

Help is available for those suffering from substance abuse, excessive drinking, or overeating:

- **Alcoholics Anonymous** aa.org offers resources for problem drinkers, family members, and friends who want to help them.

- **Al-Anon** al-anon.org is available to help if you are concerned about someone with a drinking problem.

- **Nar-Anon** nar-anon.org is a twelve-step program for family members and friends of substance abusers addicted to narcotics.

- **ACA** adultchildren.org is a twelve-step program for adult children of alcoholics and dysfunctional families.

- **Overeaters Anonymous** oa.org is a program to help individuals who have an unhealthy relationship with food and body image issues.

COPING WITH NEGATIVE EMOTIONS

When spending time with your toxic family, you will likely experience negative emotions such as anger, fear, guilt, sadness, or shame. Coping with negative emotions in a healthy manner is extremely important. You probably never learned how to process negative emotions in your family. Your family may have shamed you for expressing any feelings other than happiness. Negative emotions are often related to the negative thoughts you may be thinking about your family and yourself. In chapter 6, we will explore how to process negative thoughts.

NEGATIVE EMOTIONS EXPERIENCED IN A TOXIC FAMILY

Here are some negative emotions you may be experiencing around your toxic family:

- Abandonment
- Anger or rage
- Betrayal
- Fear
- Guilt
- Helplessness
- Hopelessness
- Isolation
- Neglect
- Resentment
- Sadness
- Self-hatred
- Shame
- Worthlessness

You can learn to manage your negative emotions in a healthy manner using the RAIN technique created by Michelle McDonald, an American meditation instructor:

- R: Recognize

- A: Allow
- I: Investigate
- N: No identification

RECOGNIZE

The first step in recognizing a negative emotion is to observe the feeling you are experiencing. Once you realize you are experiencing a negative emotion, you can try to name the feeling. If your family was like mine, the only emotions you were allowed to express were happy, sad, or mad. However, there is a multitude of emotions your body is capable of experiencing, and each one tells you something different about yourself and the world around you. To learn more about the vast array of emotions you may be experiencing, you can Google "Plutchik's Wheel of Emotions." This tool, created by psychologist Robert Plutchik, is extremely helpful while learning to process the many emotions you are capable of experiencing.

ALLOW

Allow the emotion. By naming and identifying your negative feelings, you can sit with the emotion and allow it to be. You don't have to fight what you feel, just "Let It Be," as the Beatles song says. The healthiest approach is always to face your pain rather than avoid it. When you are angry, for example, rather than demonizing your anger and labeling it as "bad," it is better to allow your anger to exist. This is called sitting with your feelings. Once you have accepted your negative emotion by allowing it to be, you can then take steps to manage your feelings in ways that do not harm others. Your family may have taught you to judge, suppress, and ignore your negative emotions instead of allowing them and managing them in a healthy manner.

In mindfulness, which we will discuss at more length in chapter 6, you do not judge your negative emotions as "bad" or something to be suppressed. You allow and accept your negative emotions as your current reality. This is called acceptance. Acceptance must always occur before you can make a change to improve your situation. Instead of numbing your negative feelings or distracting yourself with a new activity or thought, you can allow the negative emotion to be. Don't rush to fix or ignore your negative emotions.

INVESTIGATE

Instead of judging yourself or blaming others for causing your negative feelings, you can ask yourself, "What is my body trying to teach me about myself and the world around me with this negative emotion?" Let your negative emotions become your teacher. When you investigate, you do not judge but are curious. You ask yourself questions about what you are experiencing and feeling:

- Is there anything happening in my life that might be causing this feeling?
- Is there a thought I keep thinking that is causing this emotion?
- What do I need?
- Where in my body am I feeling this emotion?
- What do I need to learn about life?
- The last time I experienced this feeling, how did I cope with it in a healthy manner?

While investigating, be gentle and kind toward yourself. Show yourself compassion and loving-kindness. Investigating helps you to get in touch with your pain in ways that are not self-condemning and without blaming yourself, circumstances, or other people.

No Identification

While experiencing powerful negative emotions, remember you are not your emotions. While your body is feeling the feelings, they are not you. When you feel angry, your identity is not anger. Anger is only a fleeting feeling you are experiencing. Ten minutes or an hour from now, you won't be angry anymore. Your identity is never found in your emotions. Feelings come and go, and although they feel like they are you, they aren't. "I am feeling mad" is more accurate than "I am mad." You are never your emotion and do not need to find your identity in your feelings. You are so much more than thoughts and feelings.

In this step, you begin to find space and distance between yourself and your emotions. Eventually, every powerful negative feeling will pass, even though your mind tells you the feeling will remain forever as your permanent condition. Whenever you experience negative feelings, you can use the RAIN technique to work through them in healthy ways without losing yourself in the emotion.

Chapter Two Summary

The second step to surviving your toxic family and reclaiming your life after toxic parents is to learn healthy coping behaviors and strategies. In this chapter, we discussed healthy strategies for spending time with your unhealthy family and how to replace unhealthy coping behaviors with healthy ones. We explored substance abuse, excessive drinking, overeating, and how to cope with negative emotions. In chapter 3, we will discuss cutting ties with toxic family members.

CHAPTER 3

—⚜—

WHEN TO CUT TIES & WALK AWAY

> The moment you start to wonder if you
> deserve better, you do.
> —DAVID WILLIAMS

The third step to surviving your toxic family & reclaiming your life after toxic parents is to know when to cut ties and walk away from toxic family members.

Now that you've identified that your family is toxic and learned some healthy ways to cope with them, you're ready to face the big question, "Should I walk away and cut ties with specific harmful family members?" We will discuss this question in depth since it is a life-altering decision. In your gut, you may already know what you need to do to take care of yourself.

In this chapter, we will explore the following:

1. Journal Part III: Escape

2. Making the Decision to Walk Away

3. 4 Options for Dealing with Toxic Family

4. Issues to Consider Before Walking Away

Journal Part III: Escape

As far back as I can remember, I wanted to escape my toxic family. My bedroom was my panic room, where I ran away to hide from my family. My father regularly invaded my privacy in my room, despite it being my only safe place. He would barge in at any time, day or night and scream and yell at me for things he thought I did.

In my room, I loved to enter an imaginary world where everyone was happy and nothing ever went wrong. I mostly played with Matchbox and Hot Wheels cars. The fathers in my fictional world loved their sons and didn't punish them for being themselves.

Other than the limited privacy of my room, I had no private space in my toxic home. There was no place I could relax, unwind, and recharge my batteries. I was always hypervigilant and alert because my father had disrespected my privacy so many times before. I had no place to reflect or figure out what was happening to me. My unattainable goal was to be the perfect child, stay out of trouble, and remain invisible.

I used food to escape, make me happy, and numb my pain. If my tummy was full, I was happy. The "parent-approved" coping mechanism in our family was overeating. There was no shame in getting a second or third helping, and my entire family struggled with overeating. Rather than eating a serving of ice cream, my family ate the whole half-gallon. Even though kids at school called me "fatty" and "lard-ass," my parents never judged that part of me. Whenever I ate, I often ate until I felt sick.

Our family once visited an all-you-can-eat buffet restaurant for dinner. I always feared my father would make a scene and abuse the waitstaff based on his past horrible behavior at restaurants. I can't even count how many times he stormed out of a restaurant halfway through a meal without paying because of some perceived mistreatment or invalidation from the staff. "This time would be different," I told myself, because the restaurant was an all-you-can-eat buffet and self-serve. I was pleasantly surprised to see my dad in such a good mood throughout the entire meal. Nothing went wrong on this family outing, which was rare indeed.

What made the meal unforgettable was the fact that I ate six plates of food. As soon as I finished one plate, I got a new one and placed the dirty one on the table beside ours. By the end of the evening, I had arranged six dirty dishes on the table next to ours, as if another family had eaten there. The staff member saw the soiled dishes and asked my parents if the party next to us had finished eating and gone home.

My parents never shamed me for eating enough plates to fill a table. Instead, they thought it was hilarious the employee attributed my dirty dishes to an imaginary family of six. They laughed about that story for years, but looking back, it was a sad and cautionary tale of how I overate to soothe my emotional pain and how my parents didn't seem to mind. A little boy eating six dinner plates would be a red flag to any healthy family, but it became a punchline for mine.

In addition to playing cars and eating to escape my toxic family, I read, watched TV and movies, and played with the neighbor kids. The more time I spent with other families, the more I began to realize something was terribly wrong with my family.

When I turned nine, I became increasingly uncomfortable with the lack of privacy in my home. The bathroom door on the main floor of our house had a broken lock, so the only indication someone was using the bathroom was the closed door. I cannot count the number of times my father barged in on me while I was using the bathroom as a young boy. His intrusions always made me feel startled, violated, unsettled, and uncomfortable.

Instead of politely saying, "Oh, I'm sorry, I didn't know anyone was in the bathroom," he would say, "Hurry up, I need to pee!" and stand outside the door while he waited for me to finish. By the time I was in high school, I had developed a social phobia making it difficult for me to use public restrooms, which took years to overcome.

I wish I could go back in time and set a boundary with my father, "Please respect my privacy when I am in the bathroom. Please knock and wait your turn when the door is closed." Sadly, I suspect he would have felt threatened by such a statement and would have screamed, "Get the hell out of there because I'm waiting right here until you do."

In high school, I began drinking alcohol and smoking weed to cope with my problems. My best friend's dad, who lived on Alki Beach in West Seattle, gave us marijuana and didn't mind if we smoked it around him. He also let us drink Everclear, which is 190-proof grain alcohol. Weed and Everclear quickly helped me forget my family problems until the alcohol and drugs wore off. I didn't like weed because it made me feel paranoid and paralyzed with fear, but I smoked it anyway to get a buzz. I never drank or got high on school nights because I knew a good education was my ticket to freedom.

Doing well in school and extracurricular activities was another way to escape. My performance in school was always excellent, and

I busied myself with activities that kept me away from home. I was the drama club president, wrote a school newspaper column, sang in the barbershop quartet, and sorted nuts and bolts for a local airline manufacturer part-time. In my senior year, I directed the school play, *Our Town*, but my parents wouldn't let me go to any of the performances because they said I was "overdoing it."

I always hoped a knight in shining armor would come and rescue me from my family. But nobody ever came. Even though my situation could have been significantly worse, I realized from an early age I had to save myself if I was going to survive. Neighbors must have heard regular shouting from my house, and extended family members witnessed my father's alcohol abuse, but no one ever asked, "How is the kid doing?" Their lack of concern always baffled me but reinforced my belief that nobody would ever come to my rescue.

Years later, a relative who was my childhood babysitter told me how frightened she was of my father's drunken rage even though she never said a word. When I was an adult, I told one of my cousins the real story of what happened growing up in my family. He found the truth hard to believe and responded, "You always seemed like such a happy family."

WHEN TO CUT TIES & WALK AWAY

MAKING THE DECISION TO WALK AWAY

There is no winning in a toxic relationship; sometimes, the only way to win is not to play. Sometimes the only thing you can do to survive your toxic family and reclaim your life is to walk away from a harmful situation. David Williams wrote, "The moment you start to wonder if you deserve better, you do." If you begin to question whether you need to end the relationship after exhausting all other options, it may be time to walk away.

Getting an unhealthy family member to change their harmful behavior is difficult, if not impossible, especially when they don't think they have a problem. To live your authentic life, you must walk away from people who do not accept or support you and constantly attempt to manipulate, control, and change you. To remain in a relationship with a toxic family member, they must stop harming you, communicate openly and honestly, and respect you just as you are.

If you feel guilty about cutting ties with a family member who is harming you or wondering if it is the right thing to do, remember this: even though you may be burning the bridge, you didn't start the fire. When you begin to think about making this life-altering decision, you might second-guess yourself:

- "Maybe it's all my fault."
- "Maybe things will get better if I wait and see."
- "Maybe terrible things will happen to me if I walk away."
- "Maybe I will end up homeless and penniless."

Nobody can make this important decision for you. If you are considering cutting ties with a family member, you can ask friends and family for their opinions, but only you can make this difficult decision. Understand that walking away is not a quick fix to solve all your problems. One of the most challenging things you will ever do is to walk away from a toxic relationship.

Important note: Seek help immediately if you feel unsafe, are being abused, or are experiencing domestic violence in your family.

4 Options for Dealing with Toxic Family

If you are currently in a damaging and harmful family relationship, you have four options:

1. **Take no action:** Take no action which may further harm your emotional and physical health and well-being.

2. **Confront the toxic family member:** Confront the toxic family member or decide not to confront them for your own safety.

3. **Emotionally detach:** Maintaining healthy emotional detachment from harmful people requires letting go of them emotionally and staying safe. You can be in a relationship without disclosing private information about your life. Always remove toxic people from your inner circle. Never remain in an intimate relationship with a toxic person who is unwilling to change. (See chapter 4.)

4. **Cut ties and walk away:** Cut ties entirely and walk away from unhealthy family members.

Issues to Consider Before Walking Away

Consider these factors before walking away from a toxic family relationship:

1. Don't avoid life lessons or run away from yourself.

Walking away from a loved one means walking away from a part of yourself. When you cut ties with someone, you may be avoiding essential life lessons, such as how to deal with conflict, how to communicate with difficult people, and how to be around strong-willed people. If you don't learn these lessons now, you will need to learn them later in life. Life has much to teach you about yourself. Your teachers are often your internal struggles, challenging relationships, and roadblocks you experience in life. Running from life lessons and not accepting reality will eventually lead to suffering. Cutting ties with a family member may cut short lessons you need to learn about yourself. Although this is not a reason to remain in an unhealthy relationship, whatever lesson this relationship is supposed to teach you about yourself may be put on hold by walking away.

2. WORK THROUGH YOUR GRIEF & LOSS.

When you walk away from a loved one, no matter how harmful or abusive, you will always experience grief. Grief is a powerful sadness that occurs when there is a loss in life. You experience loss when someone you love dies or when something you care about is no longer in your life. When we lose someone, we feel grief, a painful, overwhelming, and overpowering emotion. Cutting ties with a family member has been likened to losing a loved one to death, for the grief and pain of the loss can be similar and remain for a lifetime.

Elisabeth Kübler-Ross, in her book *On Death and Dying*, introduced five stages of grief. Her research was based on patients experiencing life-threatening illnesses and the stages they experienced to process their own grief. According to Kübler-Ross, the stages of grief are as follows:

1. Denial

2. Anger

3. Bargaining

4. Depression

5. Acceptance

You will experience all the stages of grief when you cut ties with a toxic family member, and they will happen over time and not necessarily in the above order. When you think you have worked through one stage, something will trigger your grief and remind you of your broken relationship, and emotions you thought you had already processed will once again rise to the surface. Some people cover the pain of their grief and loss with anger because anger makes them feel like they have control when there is none. Know that your anger is an expression of your pain. Whether you remain in a toxic relationship or walk away from it, there will be grieving, and your grief can last a lifetime.

3. OTHER PEOPLE MAY HAVE STRONG REACTIONS

Family and friends are integral parts of your life. When you cut ties with a family member, other family members and friends may strongly react to your estrangement. Siblings, cousins, aunts and uncles, and grandparents may want you to reconcile with your toxic family member to restore the family to how it was, even if it was unhealthy. Some family members may even cut ties with you if they don't believe you are treating the estranged family member respectfully or appropriately. Similarly, friends may be critical of your decision to cut ties with a parent or sibling. In a toxic family, your survival is always more important than preserving your reputation or the honor of the family. If friends or family believe "family is sacred," they may judge you, and your relationship with them may change because they may feel you have disrespected the sanctity of the family. While you should not remain in a toxic relationship to avoid the reactions of others, cutting ties with a family member can affect many of your intimate relationships in ways you might not expect.

4. THERE WILL BE LOOSE ENDS.

Whenever you end a relationship with a loved one, there will always remain unresolved issues and irreconciled differences. For years you may feel like there are loose ends: issues you wish you could have resolved, things you wish you had told them, or complaints you wish they had heard. Even if you never want to speak with them or see them again, there may be issues you wish you could have resolved, which causes a lack of closure in the relationship. Sharing your thoughts and feelings with a trusted friend or therapist can help you deal with the ambiguities left behind by a broken relationship.

5. AVOID WALKING AWAY AS A BEHAVIOR PATTERN

Once you walk away from a toxic relationship, you may be tempted later in life to cut off everyone who upsets you or with whom you have serious disagreements. Although you may need to cut ties with an unhealthy family member, you must learn how to manage conflict, disputes, and differences in healthy relationships. Walking away must never become your go-to solution for dealing with all relationship difficulties.

WARNING SIGNS YOU MAY NEED TO CUT TIES

The following are warning signs you may need to walk away from an unhealthy family member:

- You feel insecure.
- You feel unloved.

- You feel unsafe.

- You do not feel valued.

- You do not trust the family member.

- The family member is abusing you or is domestically violent. (Take immediate action if you are in an abusive or violent home.)

- The family member blames you for everything wrong with the relationship.

- The family member blames you for their weaknesses and problems.

- The family member controls your finances or treats you like a servant.

- The family member disrespects and violates your privacy.

- The family member does not accept you unconditionally and points out all the ways you need to change.

- The family member does not accept your authentic self or creates an environment where you are not free to be who you are.

- The family member does not accept your sexual orientation or gender identity.

- The family member has demonstrated their inability or unwillingness to change their harmful behavior.

- The family member is gaslighting you by telling you your interpretation of what is happening is untrue or you are overreacting.

- The family member isolates you from support systems such as family, friends, church, or employment.

- The family member is manipulating and controlling you.

- The family member is unreliable and keeps breaking promises in ways that hurt you.

- The family member uses religion or Bible verses to shame, manipulate, control, or justify abuse and mistreatment.

- The family member struggles with addiction in ways that harm you.

REASONS PEOPLE REMAIN IN TOXIC RELATIONSHIPS

There are many reasons why people remain in toxic relationships when they are better off walking away from them or keeping the unhealthy person at a safe distance. You can cope with some dysfunctional relationships by setting boundaries, practicing self-care, and implementing healthy coping strategies, but sometimes walking away is your only healthy and safe option.

People remain in toxic relationships for the following reasons:

ABUSE SEEMS NORMAL

Some people remain in abusive relationships because the abuse they experience every day seems normal to them. As a result of growing up in an abusive family or living in an abusive relationship for many years, you might not know what a healthy relationship looks or feels like. Abuse may seem normal to you, and you may not even know a family member is abusive. I lived in a toxic family for many years before I learned there was something seriously wrong with my family. I wrongly assumed all families mistreated their children, until I began to spend time around healthy families.

FAMILY IS SACRED

Some believe the family is sacred and must be protected at all costs. They believe family honor is the most important thing in the world. Phrases like, "Family always comes first," "Family will always be there for you," "You don't turn your back on family," and, "Family is forever," are rarely said by someone who is being abused by their family.

PROTECT THE CHILDREN

Some people remain in destructive relationships for the sake of their children. They fear leaving an unhealthy relationship may result in homelessness or a lack of financial resources to care for their children. They also fear losing custody. An abusive relationship can become life-threatening and lead to long-term emotional and psychological damage for children and spouses who remain in them.

DISAPPROVAL OF FAMILY AND FRIENDS

Some people remain in dysfunctional and harmful relationships because they are worried about the disapproval of their family or friends. No one wants to be judged by their friends or families. When people who care about you and have your back discover you are in a damaging relationship, you may be surprised by their willingness to come alongside you.

FEAR OF PUNISHMENT

Some people remain in abusive relationships because they fear punishment, injury, or death if they leave a domestically violent relationship. Whenever you are in a relationship with someone who punishes or harms you, you must get help immediately. People who love you are never supposed to damage you.

WANTING TO FIX PEOPLE

Some people remain in harmful relationships because they feel the need to stay and fix the unhealthy person. They may even believe staying with the abusive person is a divine calling. Whenever you remain in dangerous or abusive relationships because you think it is your responsibility to save or fix someone, this is a red flag that your relationship is in trouble. Your desire to fix others or be their savior also says something about your self-esteem. You can never change or fix others; they need to see the problem and have the desire to change.

FINANCIAL & HOUSING

Some people remain in abusive relationships because their financial and housing resources are dependent on a toxic family member. For example, a stay-at-home parent may depend financially on their spouse for housing, food, and clothing. When you are in an unhealthy and abusive relationship, fear of becoming homeless may prevent you from taking action. Resources may be available for you by contacting the National Domestic Violence Hotline: thehotline.org.

LONELINESS

Some people remain in damaging relationships because they are afraid of being lonely. There is a difference between being lonely and being alone. Being alone means you are by yourself. Feeling lonely is a story you tell yourself, which evokes negative emotions and results in negative thinking and overthinking. If your heart and intuition tell you to get out of a relationship, fear of loneliness must never be the reason to stay.

Religion

Some people remain in unhealthy or abusive relationships because they believe their religion does not support divorce. They choose to stay in an unhealthy marriage even though it is abusive, harmful, and dangerous. A religious leader can provide guidance whenever you are in a domestically violent, harmful, or abusive relationship and are concerned about the spiritual consequences of leaving the relationship. You must be completely honest and tell them precisely what is happening in the relationship. My mother met with several pastors about her domestically violent relationship with my father. She may not have told the ministers the whole truth or ignored their advice because she never left my father's side. If your religious leader tells you to stay in an abusive or domestically violent relationship, get a second opinion.

How to Cut Ties with Toxic Family Members

Get help immediately if you have been abused or victimized by domestic violence. If you are not in danger, but the relationship is harmful and damaging to you, here are the essential steps to take when walking away from a toxic family member:

1. Assess the person's willingness to change.

2. Develop a safety plan.

3. Develop a support network of safe and accepting people

1. ASSESS THE PERSON'S WILLINGNESS TO CHANGE

Before cutting ties and walking away from an unhealthy relationship, you can assess the person's willingness to change. To make this assessment, you must let them know your concerns about their behavior and how they need to treat you from now on. If a confrontation is too dangerous for you, you may need to decide whether you believe a toxic family member can change based on your past experience with them.

If you decide to confront your family member, statements like, "You hurt my feelings," or, "You are hurting me," may trigger them and result in anger or violence. "You" statements almost always put a confronted person on the defensive, leading to a fight rather than fostering healthy dialogue. Instead, you can use "I" statements and let the other person know how their behavior makes you feel and what you need, putting the focus on what you need rather than what they are doing wrong.

By confronting your family members with a less threatening I-focused statement, you may be more effectively able to communicate with them and assess their willingness and ability to change. Once your family member understands your concerns over their behavior, if you are not in danger, you can wait and see if they are able and willing to change. If change does not occur and the harmful behavior continues, you need to decide whether to walk away from the relationship or keep them at a safe distance. Never put yourself at risk or in harm's way if you feel unsafe confronting your family member.

2. DEVELOP A SAFETY PLAN

For your own well-being when walking away from a harmful family member, you can prepare a detailed safety plan for walking away and caring for yourself during the transition. The National Domestic Violence Hotline website has a safety plan you can complete online at thehotline.org. This step-by-step plan details all the critical information you will need to walk away, including how to talk to your family and friends, contact information, and how to cope emotionally, as well as resources available to assist you.

3. DEVELOP A SUPPORT NETWORK OF SAFE & ACCEPTING PEOPLE

The best way to cut ties and walk away from an unhealthy relationship is to surround yourself with people who love, accept, and support you. Abusive or harmful people must never be a part of your inner circle. (See chapter 4, "Remove Toxic People from Your Inner Circle.")

WALKING AWAY FROM RELIGIOUS ABUSE

Religious abuse can be committed by an individual, group, or organization, such as a Bible study or church. Often religious abusers justify their abuse because they think they are trying to teach you a spiritual lesson, believe the end justifies the means, or think they're helping God do God's work. Religious abuse may leave you wondering if you should walk away from the person or organization, change churches, or leave the religion altogether. The good news is that you can still believe in God and not spend time around religiously abusive people.

Religious abuse, also known as spiritual abuse or religious trauma, can take many forms:

1. Emotional

2. Financial

3. Physical

4. Psychological

5. Sexual

6. Spiritual

7. Verbal

EXAMPLES OF RELIGIOUS ABUSE

The following are examples of different types of religious abuse:

- Using religion or Bible verses to shame, manipulate, control, humiliate, ridicule, or embarrass rather than love individuals

- Using religion or Bible verses to excuse or justify domestic violence and abuse

- Forcing someone to do things against their will, including giving money or having unwanted sexual relations

- Forcing someone to practice or follow a particular religion or spiritual belief against their will

- Forcing someone to stay in an unhealthy or abusive marriage

- Preventing family members from getting medical or psychological care

- Rigid, dogmatic, judgmental, and unaccepting approach to others based on religious views

- Shaming or punishing others for their sexual orientation or gender identity based on religious views

- Shaming or punishing others for their religious or spiritual beliefs

- Treating women or other people as subordinates based on religious views

Guilt is about what you did wrong, while shame is about what is fundamentally wrong with you. Shame is about non-acceptance and self-hatred. Shame is the most frequent side effect of religious abuse. Whenever my parents asked me, "What's wrong with you?" after I made a mistake, I felt shame rather than guilt. Feeling less than, unworthy, not enough, flawed, evil, judged, and unloved can be symptoms of spending time with a religious abuser.

SYMPTOMS OF RELIGIOUS ABUSE

The following are some symptoms of religious abuse:

- Addictions
- Anxiety
- Difficulty trusting others and forming relationships
- Extreme self-criticism, self-hatred, or self-loathing
- Hopelessness and depression
- Hypervigilance (anxiety due to constantly assessing threats around you or trying to be perfect to meet strict religious standards or requirements)
- Identity crisis or identity development issues (The individual struggles to form an identity due to the strict religious rules or the overwhelming influence of the religious institution.)
- Isolation and lack of community if ostracized by the church or religious family members
- Lack of self-confidence

- Low self-esteem

- Obsessive-compulsive

- Perfectionism

- Post-traumatic stress (PTSD)

- Strong feelings of guilt and shame

- Sexual dysfunction (belief that sex in specific contexts is evil, especially unmarried, non-heterosexual, or non-procreative sexual practices)

- Sexual identity or gender identity crisis

- Unhealthy boundaries (difficulty determining where one person ends and another person begins, a compulsion to confess secrets, make public things they wish to remain private)

- Worry

Religious abuse almost always begins with the abuser's subconscious belief they need to play the role of God and judge, shame others, or teach someone a lesson. Whenever someone judges or shames another person, they are inappropriately meddling in God's business. Human beings have no place judging or shaming one another. Almost every weakness someone sees in others stems from an unresolved internal conflict or hypocrisy. A religious person is better off leaving judgment to God and making it their aim to love people. If anyone thinks God needs their help to shame and judge others, their faith isn't strong enough, and their God isn't big enough. If every religious person loved the way their religion taught them, there would be no religious abuse.

OVERCOMING RELIGIOUS ABUSE

The following are helpful strategies to overcome religious abuse:

- Set boundaries: Walk away from or create a safe distance between yourself and the abuser. Take a break to gain perspective from an institution you believe is doing you more harm than good.

- Develop a safe and accepting support group: Find non-judgmental, supporting people who accept you just as you are.

- Journaling: Record your thoughts and feelings to gain perspective.

- Mindfulness and meditation: Focus on being non-judgmental about yourself and others and gaining perspective.

- Religious organization: If a religious organization causes you anguish or trauma, take a break from the religious organization until you decide whether to remain in the organization, join another religious organization, or stop attending religious organizations entirely. Never affiliate with an organization that does not fundamentally accept you just as you are. Get an opinion from a person you trust before returning to the organization.

- Religious person: Maintain your distance from a religious person if they caused you anguish or trauma while you decide whether to remain in the relationship at a safe distance or walk away. Never spend extended time with people who do not fundamentally accept you just as you are.

- Self-care: Focus on taking care of yourself first, reducing your anxiety, and relaxing.

- Spirituality: When you feel ready, spend time thinking about what you believe and what kind of spirituality you wish to practice, if any.

- Therapy: Consult a therapist and consider one not affiliated with the religion in question.

If someone is using religion to abuse, shame, or control you, as soon as possible, get help, walk away, or keep them at a safe distance.

WALKING AWAY FROM LGBTQ+ DISCRIMINATION

Coping with sexual orientation and gender identity issues in a toxic family can be traumatizing. Many LGBTQ+ people, especially those under eighteen, remain in toxic and abusive family relationships where harassment occurs daily. LGBTQ+ individuals often hide their true identity for fear of abandonment or homelessness if they reveal their sexual orientation or gender identity. Sadly, some religious families would rather force non-heterosexual or gender-nonconforming children out of the house rather than accept and love them for who they are. Even if it means the homeless child must resort to prostitution or selling drugs to survive, some religious people view this as a just punishment for their sins.

A healthy family helps family members navigate the often-confusing waters of sexual orientation and gender identity with love and acceptance, not judgment. A healthy family practices no discrimination against sexual orientation or gender identity. They are not homophobic (prejudiced against LGBTQ+ people) or transphobic (biases or prejudiced against transgender people). They do not view heterosexuality as the normative sexual orientation (heterosexism).

If you are experiencing sexual orientation or gender identity discrimination in your family, contact the Trevor Project 24/7/365:

- thetrevorproject.org
- LGBTQ+ crisis counseling and suicide prevention
- TrevorSpace – Community for LGBTQ+ young people (ages thirteen to twenty-four); affirming online community with answers to questions (sexual orientation, gender identity, mental health, and more)

If you are LGBTQ+ or are struggling with what the Bible teaches about homosexuality, here are two books I would recommend reading:

- *Changing Our Mind: Definitive 3rd Edition of the Landmark Call for Inclusion of LGBTQ Christians with Response to Critics,* David P. Gushee
- *God and the Gay Christian: The Biblical Case in Support of Same-Sex Relationships,* Matthew Vines

You must never be ashamed of who you are. If someone is harming you or discriminating against you because you are an LGBTQ+ person, get help as soon as possible, walk away, or keep them at a safe distance.

CHAPTER THREE SUMMARY

The third step to surviving your toxic family and reclaiming your life after toxic parents is to know when to cut ties and walk away from toxic family members. In this chapter, we explored making the decision to walk away, warning signs, why people remain in toxic relationships, how to walk away, and walking away from religious abuse and LGBTQ+ discrimination. In chapter 4, we will discuss how to set healthy boundaries and build healthy relationships.

Chapter 4

— ❧ —

Boundaries & Healthy Relationships

Don't settle for a relationship that won't let
you be yourself.

—Oprah Winfrey

**The fourth step to surviving your toxic family & reclaiming
your life after toxic parents is to set healthy boundaries
and build healthy relationships.**

Whether you decide to walk away from a toxic family member or keep them at a safe distance, healthy boundaries are one of the foundations of all healthy relationships. In this chapter, you will learn how to set strong boundaries with difficult family members and surround yourself with like-minded people who have your back, are on your side, and accept you as you are.

In this chapter, we will explore the following:

1. Journal Part IV: Broken Relationships

2. Setting Healthy Boundaries

3. Types of Healthy Boundaries

4. Strong Boundary Statements

5. Removing Toxic People from Your Inner Circle

6. Breaking Unhealthy Relationship Patterns

JOURNAL PART IV: BROKEN RELATIONSHIPS

Much of my life has been marked by broken and unhealthy relationships. The dysfunctional behaviors I learned from my toxic family spilled over into other significant relationships outside my family. My relationship with my father was by far the most destructive relationship I have ever experienced. The way he treated me left me with lifelong emotional scars.

In our family, internal boundaries were non-existent. A *relationship boundary* is a healthy separation between where you stop and where others start. When people get too involved in your personal business, you may feel they are violating your boundaries. My dad claimed he had extra sensory perception (ESP) and could read my mind. Often, he would say, "Don't lie, or I'll know." His words implied he knew the private contents of my thoughts and would punish me if he ever caught me lying. Any child who believes his dad has the power to get inside his head will end up emotionally and psychologically damaged. Consequently, not even my mind was a safe space. By the time I realized he was being psychologically abusive, I was already seriously damaged.

At nine years old, I believed that something was fundamentally wrong with my relationship with my father, and he would never be the man I had hoped he would be. My relationship with my dad always seemed strained and distant. My entire life, we only participated in three father-son activities together.

Father-Son Activity #1. One summer morning, my dad asked me if I wanted to go out to breakfast alone with him. My dad asking me to go to breakfast was not his typical behavior, so I was curious and suspicious.

"OK, sure," I said intrepidly.

We drove to the Denny's near SeaTac airport. I remember it like it was yesterday because it was the first time we had done anything together, just the two of us. We sat at the counter because the restaurant was completely full. I was glad we didn't have to sit face-to-face. Even as a kid, I knew face-to-face eye contact with my dad would be weird.

When the waitress came to take our order, Dad said, "Order anything you want, Son."

I looked at him and thought to myself, "Who is this alien sitting next to me, and what have you done with my father?"

"I'll take the blueberry waffles with whipped cream."

"Fill it to the sky with whipped cream," he told the waitress. "Don't be stingy."

The waitress smiled and put our order on the spinning stainless steel order wheel for the cooks. I remember thinking this was "cool" and "fun," but then I realized my dad was smiling but not talking. I hoped the food would come fast to break the silence. Soon, the waitress arrived with a massive plate of waffles with more whipped cream than I had ever seen.

"Wow. Thanks!" I looked at the waitress and my dad to acknowledge them both.

I don't remember if my dad ordered any food. I was too busy inhaling the blueberry waffles with whipped cream. After I ate about three-quarters, I began to feel sick to my stomach.

"Are you done, champ?" my dad broke the silence and asked.

"Yes, I think so."

He said, "Good job," to me and to the waitress. "Can we have the check?"

After paying and while we were walking out the door, my father put his arm around me. I looked at my dad with awe and wonder. Was it possible my dad was really cool and I didn't know it? Could this be the start of something amazing? My dad looked at me before we got into the car, pointed at a smudge of whipped cream still on my face, and smiled. I wiped off the whipped cream, and we drove home in total silence. When we got home, I said, "Thanks for the waffles."

"No problem, champ," he said and hung up his coat.

I could tell nothing had changed between my dad and me in the days that followed. We still had nothing in common and nothing to say to each other. Our relationship remained strained and distant.

Father-Son Activity #2. Our second breakfast alone together was at a restaurant called Tommy's Cafe in Renton a few months later. I ordered eggs sunny side up, sausage links, and sourdough toast. Next to the strawberry jam on the table, there was a jar of what looked like orange jam.

"What's this?" I asked.

He perked up. "You've got to try this. It's called marmalade. You'll love it. My aunts served me marmalade for breakfast when I was a kid your age. Did you know they were co-valedictorians of their class at West Seattle High School?"

I could tell my dad was trying to improve our relationship. He was right about the marmalade; it was delicious. When I finished my last bite, our second father-son activity ended with the same awkward silence. I often pondered what our relationship might have looked like if I had been talented in sports or if we had a shared hobby. I wondered how different my childhood would have been if we had kicked a ball around or watched a game together, things we never did. We only had one thing in common—our love of food.

Father-Son Activity #3. The third and final father-son activity of my life ended in complete disaster. My mom, dad, and I went camping in the Cascade Mountains. On the first day of our trip, my parents spent most of the day riding my dad's motorcycle, leaving me alone to hang out around the campsite.

On the second day of the trip, my dad asked, "How about a motorcycle ride, just you and me?"

I knew this would end badly and didn't want to go. Against my better judgment, I said, "Sure, OK," because I wanted to please him and I thought a son ought to do stuff with his dad.

My dad started up his 1972 Harley Davidson Rapido. I climbed on the back, and he said, "No matter what happens, don't shift your weight. Just hold on tight to me and don't move."

At first, I thought it was cool I was holding onto my dad as we rode this loud little motorcycle through the woods. Suddenly the paved road turned to loose gravel. On a very sharp corner, the motorcycle slid out from underneath us, and we both went down with the bike. After the crash, I saw that the motorcycle had a few scratches, and my dad seemed OK. My leg was cut badly by the jagged gravel rocks. What hurt more than my wounds was the thought, "Somehow, this is going to be my fault. I'm going to be punished for this."

My dad checked over the bike, looked at me, and then said sternly, "This was all your fault. You shifted your weight, which made us go down."

He didn't seem to care or notice my bloodied leg and ripped pants. "How could this be my fault?" I thought. "And who cares whose fault it is? The bike is fine, and we're both alive." Angry and without another word, he got back on the motorcycle, started it up, and rode away, leaving me on the gravel road. I limped back to the campsite. This was our last father-son activity ever. In the following nine years, until he kicked me out of the house, we rarely spoke directly to each other. I could tell my father was done trying to make our relationship work. I was done too. I also think he was done being a father and regretted having children in the first place.

When I was nine years old, my relationship with my mom took a turn for the worse. My mom called me into her bedroom while my dad was away at work. She asked me to sit beside her on the bed. She burst into tears and said, "Nothing I do is good enough for your dad." She shared how unhappy she was in her marriage and how she was thinking about leaving my dad. She asked, "Why does your dad mistreat me when all I do is love him, keep the house clean, and put a hot meal on the table three times a day?"

Then she asked me the million-dollar question: "Do you think I should leave him?"

"Yes!" I answered in a heartbeat.

My mother shared her most intimate thoughts and feelings about my father's drinking and abusive behavior. She talked about leaving him, but she never did. I served as her confidant, surrogate spouse, and amateur therapist for almost two years. I would later learn what I already knew in my heart: making a child a confidant, called parentification, is a subtle form of child abuse.

What bothered me most about those times in her bedroom was she never once asked me how I was doing or how my father's abuse and domestic violence affected me. Soon, I realized my only ally seemed unaware of my suffering. Her tears were always about her pain and never mine. As a result of my mother's dependency on me for emotional support at the expense of my needs, I felt hopeless.

Depression began to set in when I believed the only person who could save me didn't even seem concerned about how I was doing.

One afternoon in her bedroom, my mom confessed that she feared my dad might physically harm her. Suddenly, I felt the need to protect her. I always felt threatened and unsafe around my father. That afternoon, I vowed to kill him if he ever hurt my mom. Thank God he never physically hurt my mom or me.

Even though she made me her confidant, my relationship with my mom was the only thing that kept my childhood from being a total nightmare. While I loved my mom, I was always bewildered why she never confronted my dad about his abuse and domestic violence. She never walked away from him and took me with her. She believed the Bible taught wives to submit, honor, and obey their husbands no matter what.

My dad's alcoholic father abandoned him as a child at age four and was a horrible father to him his entire life. They reconciled in my dad's teenage years, but his dad was drunk most nights. Given that my father had such a terrible childhood, I always wondered why he didn't try harder to learn how to be a good dad. If I were in his shoes, I would have read every book on how to be a good father. I would have learned from experts how to raise, bond with, and love a son. Throughout my childhood, I always wondered why he never tried very hard to be a loving father. I eventually concluded he didn't want children. I think he finally came to that conclusion himself when I turned ten. Everything would change.

One night through the thin walls of my bedroom, I heard my dad lecturing my mom late into the evening. The following day after he left for work, my mom sat me down at the kitchen table and did the unthinkable. She gave me what I have for years called "The Speech." I remember it word for word. She most likely repeated what my father had told her the night before. I always believed my mom was just a victim and not a co-conspirator in my hellish childhood. But I think I was wrong.

"I have something very important to tell you, and everything will be different from now on, beginning immediately. This is how your father wants it. As your mother, I have spent the past ten years raising you and focusing on your needs, and it has made your dad very jealous. He feels abandoned and ignored. You are now ten years old, practically a man, and you need to grow up. Starting now, I will focus all my energy on caring for your father since he feels neglected. Your dad and I will take trips alone on weekends, just the two of us, and leave you home alone with a babysitter. Everything is going to change beginning today. You're a grown-up now. My focus will be on your father from this day forward."

I held back the tears, lied, and said I understood while I quietly grieved the loss of my sad and disappointing life, family, and childhood.

BOUNDARIES & HEALTHY RELATIONSHIPS

SETTING HEALTHY BOUNDARIES

Boundaries define where one person ends and another person begins. In relationships, they express your limits and expectations and how you want others to treat you. People do not inherently know your boundaries, so you must define them clearly for others. Boundaries are also about self-respect and not allowing others to mistreat you.

In healthy families, healthy boundaries facilitate the following:

- Authentic individuality
- Conflict resolution
- Open communication
- Respect

By setting strong and healthy boundaries in toxic relationships, you are letting others know you are no longer willing to be treated in ways that harm you. Your boundaries must also align with your authentic self—who you really are. Your boundaries may not make sense to others if you are not being yourself. If you play a role or wear a false mask, what you want and need may not be evident to others.

Boundaries exist in both healthy and unhealthy families. Toxic families are either too involved in your business or are too aloof and uncaring. Boundaries may be rigid, where there is a clear and distinguishable line between individuals, or vague, where there is no clear delineation between where one person stops and another person starts.

I learned very quickly not to set boundaries in my family. I was threatened, punished, called a "snitch," or labeled a "complainer" whenever I tried to set limits. Eventually, I gave up trying to stick up for myself and tell others how I wanted to be treated, which resulted in anger, resentment, hopelessness, and despair. My family had rigid boundaries with the outside world. My father regularly instructed us not to discuss our family secrets or what went on in our house with anyone outside the family, including extended family, neighbors, and school officials. Because of our rigid boundaries, it was impossible to get help. My father discouraged external relationships and sabotaged my mother's desire to attend church or get a job.

In contrast, our internal boundaries were vague and unclear. There was no clear line between where I started and my dad stopped. My dad would regularly invade my space and privacy in every way possible. My family was totally enmeshed, and we were all excessively and inappropriately dependent on one another, negatively impacting our sense of self and self-esteem. Whenever my dad got upset, I had an immediate emotional and visceral reaction because I knew his anger or unhappiness would ultimately affect me negatively.

To establish vague and unclear internal boundaries, my father set the following family rules:

- "Don't lie to me; I can read your mind."
- "Don't keep any secrets from me."
- "Tell me everything you are thinking."
- "Keep quiet in your bedroom; we can hear everything you do up there."

To establish external boundaries, my father set the following family rules:

- "Don't talk to strangers."
- "Don't tell anyone the family secrets."
- "Trust no one outside the family, including extended family, neighbors, and school officials."
- "Watch out for all the fags and perverts."

A healthy family is neither isolated from the outside world nor entangled with or estranged from its members. When someone in a healthy family feels pain, loving family members feel sympathy or empathy but never fear for their own safety.

TYPES OF HEALTHY BOUNDARIES

Boundaries are a form of self-care and self-respect. You can set and enforce different types of boundaries to ensure healthy relationships:

- Emotional boundaries: the right to express your feelings in a manner reflecting your authentic self.

- Financial boundaries: the right to spend money as you choose and the right to receive fair compensation for your work.

- Intellectual boundaries: freedom to express your ideas and thoughts and keep information private if you prefer.

- Physical boundaries: the right to decide who touches you and how you wish to be touched.

- Sexual boundaries: the right to decide how you define yourself sexually as well as when, how often, and with whom you wish to have sexual intimacy.

- Spiritual boundaries: freedom to worship and believe as you wish or freedom not to worship.

- Time boundaries: the right to choose how you spend your time.

If someone violates your boundaries, you can say "no" or "stop," and healthy individuals will respect your limits. In a toxic family, you are unlikely to receive the respect you need and deserve. When people consistently fail to respect the boundaries you set, the relationship is unhealthy, and you either need to walk away from the individual or keep the person at a safe distance. If you try to set strong boundaries with toxic family members with anger and control issues, don't be surprised if they become angry with you or give you the silent treatment because you have threatened their false sense of control or superiority.

STRONG BOUNDARY STATEMENTS

If you have tried to set boundaries with family members and have had no success, it is time to begin using strong boundary statements if you feel it is safe to do so. When "No!" or "Stop!" doesn't work with your family members, you need to use assertive boundary statements that will clearly let them know where they stop and where you start:

- "I will end this conversation if you keep yelling at me. We can talk when you gain control of your emotions."
- "I'd rather not answer that question."
- "I'd rather not discuss that topic."
- "I'm not looking for advice on that topic right now."
- "It's not OK to abuse me."
- "It's not OK to hurt me."
- "It's not OK to keep telling me to do something when I have already said, 'No, I'm not going to do that.'"
- "It's not OK to shame me."
- "It's not OK to embarrass me and make me feel stupid."
- "It's not OK to try to control or manipulate me."
- "It's not OK to try to change me."
- "It's not OK to use religion to control or manipulate me."
- "It's not OK for you to give unsolicited advice without asking my permission."
- "It's not OK for you to raise your voice at me."
- "It's not OK for you to speak to me in that tone of voice."

When using strong boundary statements, make sure your tone and body language indicate a desire to improve the relationship and not pick a fight. Your goal is to be respectful while communicating how you want to be treated for your own self-respect.

REMOVING TOXIC PEOPLE FROM YOUR INNER CIRCLE

You never want to remain in an intimate unhealthy relationship where your emotional and psychological health, well-being, and safety are at risk. Healthy emotional detachment is when you stop sharing aspects of your personal life, what you are thinking and feeling, with toxic family members. Only spend time with people who support your authentic life, happiness, mental health, and well-being. Spend time with people you can let your hair down, relax, have fun, and be your authentic self around. Avoid people who don't accept you, who judge you, or who want to change, control, manipulate, or harm you.

As soon as you determine your family member is abusive or harmful and unwilling or incapable of change, you must immediately remove them from your inner circle and stop sharing your life with them. Removing an unhealthy person from your inner circle does not mean you cannot spend limited time with them or love them from a safe distance. You can still have relationships with unhealthy family members if they are not abusive, dangerous, or harmful.

When you exclude someone from your inner circle, you must immediately stop sharing your hopes, dreams, plans, struggles, desires, and longings with these people. People who have mistreated you in the past have no right to know the intimate details of your life. You must exclude anyone from your inner circle who doesn't accept you just as you are—your authentic self.

Oprah Winfrey wrote, "Don't settle for a relationship that won't let you be yourself." You must be your authentic self at all costs, at all times, and in all relationships. You do not need to wait for anyone's permission or approval to live your best life. You must never settle for relationships where you must change who you are to be accepted.

Your self-esteem is damaged whenever you hold back the full expression of yourself because another person doesn't accept you or wants to change you. You must not waste your life trying to please people who do not accept you just as you are. Life is too short to spend time with people who won't let you be you.

Whether you decide to cut ties and walk away from your family members or keep them at a safe distance, having safe, supportive, and healthy people around you will be an emotional safety net for you. As you begin rebuilding your self-esteem and self-confidence, you need a small group of safe and accepting people you can turn to for emotional support.

Bobcat Goldthwait wrote, "I used to think the worst thing in life was to end up all alone. It's not. The worst thing in life is ending up with people who make you feel all alone." You are better off alone than being around abusive, controlling, judgmental, manipulative, negative, and unaccepting people. Limit your closest relationships to those who accept you without judgment, don't want to change you, and love you just as you are. If your family does not love and accept you, find someone who does and create a family of your own choosing.

BREAKING UNHEALTHY RELATIONSHIP PATTERNS

You learned unhealthy relationship patterns of behavior as a result of growing up in a toxic, dysfunctional family. These behaviors do not promote healthy intimacy in relationships. You must identify these patterns and stop repeating them to have successful intimate relationships in the future.

Examples of unhealthy relationship behaviors can include the following:

- Being attracted to certain types of people (abusers, substance abusers, people who need fixing)
- Boundary issues
- Bullying
- Codependency
- Conflict resolution difficulties
- Control
- Disrespect
- Giving the silent treatment, cutting people off, or ghosting them
- Intimacy problems
- Isolation
- Jealousy
- Keeping secrets or revealing too much information
- Labeling others as superior or inferior
- Love bombs (lavishing someone with attention or gifts to control and manipulate)
- Lying
- Manipulation
- Other types of abuse and domestic violence (emotional, financial, physical, psychological, spiritual)
- Passive-aggressive behavior
- People-pleasing
- Poor communication, top-down communication, no communication

- Possessiveness
- Selfishness
- Sexual problems
- Substance abuse
- Verbal abuse, shouting, screaming, yelling

Below are three ways to break the cycle of toxic behavior in your relationships:

1. EXAMINE PAST FAILED RELATIONSHIPS

One way to break the cycle of harmful relationship behaviors is to make a chronological list of your unhealthy relationships. You can then examine the list and look for common behaviors, disappointments, and losses. Looking for patterns in your past failed relationships can be a key to unlocking the reasons why your relationships became dysfunctional and failed in the first place. You will always make mistakes in life, but it is always better to make new mistakes rather than to keep repeating the same old ones.

2. ASK TRUSTED FRIENDS AND FAMILY

Another way to break the cycle of dysfunctional behavior in relationships is to ask safe, accepting, trusted, and empathetic friends and family members if they have noticed any harmful patterns in your relationships. Remember only to ask for help from people who accept you just as you are.

3. GET HELP TO HEAL PAST TRAUMA

A therapist can assist if you are repeating unhealthy behaviors in healthy relationships. A therapist can help you learn how to stop repeating the same unhealthy relationship patterns in the future by understanding your past trauma.

CHAPTER FOUR SUMMARY

The fourth step to surviving your toxic family and reclaiming your life after toxic parents is to set healthy boundaries and build healthy relationships. In this chapter, we explored setting and enforcing strong and healthy boundaries, removing toxic people from your inner circle, and breaking unhealthy relationship patterns. In chapter 5, we will discuss how to make self-care a priority.

CHAPTER 5

— ❧ —

TAKE CARE OF YOURSELF

Self-care is not self-indulgence, it is self-preservation.
—AUDRE LORDE

The fifth step to surviving your toxic family & reclaiming your life after toxic parents is to make self-care a priority.

Making yourself a priority is something your toxic parents failed to teach you. It is impossible to care for others if you don't care for yourself. Some people think putting yourself first is selfish, but in a toxic family, it's survival. Self-care is self-love. Make sure you get the self-care you deserve!

In this chapter, we will explore the following:

1. Journal Part V: Trying to Find Myself in California

2. Self-Care After Neglect

3. Balanced Self-Care Plan

4. How to Journal

5. How to Meditate

6. Face Your Pain

7. How to Get Help When Needed

8. Coping with Depression

9. Managing PTSD

JOURNAL PART V: TRYING TO FIND MYSELF IN CALIFORNIA

Once I turned eighteen, and only a few months after graduating high school, my father gave me an ultimatum. He told me I needed to "become a part of our family and do more chores around the house or get out." I worked full-time at a hospital on First Hill in downtown Seattle to save money for college. After work, I hung out with friends to avoid dealing with family drama. Even though I knew my father was over being a dad by the time I was ten, I was shocked and angered when he finally gave me an ultimatum to shape up or move out. I had known for years this day would come. He made one final attempt to control my life, but I called his bluff.

I went to my room to plan my escape. Since I had recently been promoted to weekend supervisor at the hospital, I calculated my budget and determined I could afford to move out. The universe always has perfect timing. I checked the *Seattle Times* classified housing ads and found an apartment near the university I could afford.

The following day when I broke the news, my father seemed surprised and relieved by my decision to leave. His dream of a home without children had finally come true. My mom cried when I told her I was moving out. I was gone in less than a week and never looked back. After years of my dad's neglect and my mom's failure to stand up for me, leaving our family home was the greatest act of self-care of my entire life.

My new apartment was near Green Lake in Seattle. Shortly after moving, I was walking to the University of Washington to register for classes when suddenly I was overtaken by an overwhelming feeling of freedom. I felt an overwhelming flood of emotions as I stood on the sidewalk. I felt like crying, but I couldn't. A powerful sense of relief filled my being as if an enormous burden had been lifted. Suddenly I was free of the anxiety and dread that had plagued my childhood. I was free from my father's humiliation, bullying, belittling, and terrorizing. An overwhelming sense of joy and peace filled my heart. I was finally free of the monster. Or so I thought.

Unfortunately, freedom from my childhood home wasn't enough to magically heal years of trauma and the post-traumatic stress I was now experiencing. I began noticing social phobias, fears, and anxieties in college. It was clear to me these were remnants of my abusive childhood, but I had no idea how to deal with them. Over the next few years, I busied myself with school and got heavily involved in a Christian college ministry, where I eventually became president. Although I played the role of a good Christian leader on the outside, I felt terrified whenever anyone talked about "gays" or if anyone ever asked me about my "childhood."

When I was getting ready to graduate from university, several friends asked me to move with them to Los Angeles to start our careers. I hoped moving 1,200 miles away from my family would free me of my past. The move to California was not a mistake, but believing it would solve all my toxic family issues was.

A few months after arriving in California, I got a job at a bank in Santa Monica. Hanging out on the West side of Los Angeles and at the beach in Malibu, I started seeing actors in real life I'd grown up watching on TV and in the movies. One night, I went into a theater in Westwood and realized I was sitting next to Drew Barrymore. She said, "Hi," and we had a great time talking before the movie started. A few weeks later, I was catching a film in Los Feliz and sat directly behind Leonardo DiCaprio.

I joined the Summer Choir at Hollywood Presbyterian Church during my first summer in LA. The choir director helped me get an interview at one of the most prestigious universities in Southern California, where I would work for almost twenty years. In the choir, I met a young woman from Atlanta, Georgia, and we started hanging out. With time, we grew closer and eventually became romantically involved. Even though I was attracted to her on many levels, I was concerned about my sexual identity. I met with a friend of mine who was a minister and told him about my sexual orientation and some same-sex experiences I had in junior high and high school. He told me not to worry and said many guys have experimental experiences similar to mine.

After taking his advice, I decided to ask her to marry me. I proposed to her at the top of the Bonaventure Hotel in downtown LA and drove her home in a white Lincoln Town Car after celebratory drinks at the Polo Lounge in the Beverly Hills Hotel. We had an extravagant wedding at our church in Hollywood after being engaged for a year. Our wedding night didn't go so well. That night on the cruise ship to the Caribbean, I realized I had made an enormous mistake by ignoring my sexual identity. I hoped I could change and prayed I might be bisexual. But I wasn't.

We were married for seven years. Early on, my wife suspected I was going through something, so she recommended I see a psychiatrist. On my first visit, the doctor diagnosed me with chronic depression and prescribed antidepressants, which I took for twenty years. During the second visit, he told me I was gay and that I needed to tell my wife. Years later, my therapist would also add PTSD to my diagnosis.

My wife already knew what I had to tell her when we sat down to talk seriously. Together, we worked through the grief of our failed marriage. We cried in each other's arms for hours. Our divorce was extremely amicable, and even today, we are friends. The pain of loneliness and depression led me to drink more heavily after the divorce.

My professional life took off despite my excessive drinking, and I was promoted to one of the directors of one of the largest departments at the university. I managed a large team and worked as a professional writer and speaker, traveling the country and giving talks at student recruitment events from New York City to Honolulu. I earned a substantial wage and moved into a beautifully restored historic 1917 apartment above the Grand Central Market in downtown Los Angeles. Nicolas Cage lived in the penthouse of my building, and we had sweeping views of downtown Los Angeles.

While working at the university, I befriended a colleague in my department. He eventually moved to Montecito, California, next to Santa Barbara, and we became best friends. For several years, I worked in LA during the week and spent weekends with him in Montecito. His home had a spectacular view of the Pacific Ocean and was less than a mile from the palatial estates of Oprah and Ellen. We dined in great Santa Barbara and Montecito restaurants, drank wine, and smoked cigars on his deck. After three years, he married a young woman from his church and moved away. Those days in Montecito were some of the best days of my life.

With my traumatic childhood, a failed marriage, and the loss of a close friend, my depression worsened. The more depressed I became, the more I drank. After mixing significant quantities of chardonnay with my antidepressants, the drug eventually became ineffective. My chronic depression and alcohol abuse affected my job negatively, and I began making small but noticeable mistakes.

Instead of firing me, my bosses summoned me to a "Come to Jesus" meeting, explaining how my missteps negatively impacted my career and the university. The dean of my department sat me down and said, "If you want to keep your job at the university, you have to start taking care of yourself and get into rehab starting today."

TAKE CARE OF YOURSELF

SELF-CARE AFTER NEGLECT

Self-care is self-love. Self-care is taking care of yourself emotionally, mentally, physically, and spiritually. Your toxic family most likely never taught you how to care for yourself. In a dysfunctional family, everyone surrenders their self-care and well-being to care for the family's most unhealthy person. In my family, this was my father. These needy family members always come first, whether you like it or not. To meet their dysfunctional needs, you had to neglect yourself, especially if there was substance abuse in the family.

Like on an airplane, you must always put on your own oxygen mask first before helping others. While helping others in life is important, your family most likely did not teach you the importance of self-care and the dangers of self-neglect. In a sense, you sacrificed yourself so your toxic family members could always have their needs met. Your family failed to teach you essential survival skills and neglected your feelings, needs, wants, and desires. You may have even left your unhealthy family home without learning the necessary life skills to take care of yourself.

If you can't love or care for yourself, you will find it difficult to love and care for others. Ru Paul, the famous American drag queen, said, "If you don't love yourself, how in the hell you gonna love somebody else?" Many victims of dysfunctional families later seek codependent partners to care for them. They look to a partner to make their daily decisions and tell them what to do. Even the most loving partner, family member, or friend cannot take responsibility for your self-care. You must learn to love and care for yourself to heal from your neglectful family. Only then can you love and care for another person.

EXAMPLES OF SELF-CARE ACTIVITIES

The following are examples of self-care activities:

- Breathe normally
- Drink plenty of water (watch dehydration)
- Eat healthily
- Get plenty of exercise
- Get plenty of sleep
- Go to a coffee shop
- Go to the movies
- Journal
- Lay out in the sun
- Listen to music you like
- Meditate
- Phone/text a friend
- Pray
- Read a book
- Sip tea slowly
- Spend time with people who are easy to be around
- Take a break from electronic screens

- Take a walk in the park or the woods
- Take a warm bath or shower
- Write a list of things you are grateful for

BALANCED SELF-CARE PLAN

Living a life of self-love instead of neglect includes implementing a balanced self-care plan. A self-care plan will help you to achieve balance in the many aspects of your life: emotional, environmental, financial, mental, physical, social, and spiritual. Maintaining a sense of balance in your life is essential. Humans crave balance. You become stressed, unhappy, and sick when your life is out of balance. For example, if you work too many long hours without rest, relaxation, or fun, you will eventually become exhausted and burn out. If you neglect different aspects of your life, you will fall out of balance, and life will bring you back into harmony when you least expect it. Something will happen to force you back into balance, such as coming down with a cold or illness.

SAMPLE SELF-CARE PLAN

The following is an example of a self-care plan. You can use this as a model and customize the plan according to your own wants and needs.

EMOTIONAL

- Meditate daily and when life gets stressful or overwhelming.
- Keep a journal and document your feelings, challenges, and relationship issues.

- Observe and process negative emotions when they arise using the RAIN technique from chapter 2.

ENVIRONMENTAL

- Be a minimalist, dust, declutter, and keep the house clean and organized.
- Mow the lawn, weed the garden, and recycle your garbage.
- Decorate your walls with art, decor, and memorabilia that make you feel good.

FINANCIAL

- Develop a realistic budget and revise it as needed. Get out of debt if you can.
- Monitor your bank accounts and credit report for fraud and limit credit card spending. Pay off your credit card debt every month if you can.
- Swedish proverb: "One who buys what they do not need steals from themselves."
  —UNKNOWN.

MENTAL

- Be creative: draw, paint, write, sing, and enjoy music.
- Engage in positive self-talk by focusing on positive core beliefs about yourself (see chapter 6):
  - I am more than enough.
  - I am lovable, just as I am, and worthy of self-love.

- I can be OK even if everyone around me isn't.

- I have everything I need for now.

- It's going to get easier.

- I've got this.

- Engage in activities that stimulate your mind, like reading, crossword puzzles, or word puzzles.

PHYSICAL

- Exercise daily, walk when you can, and take stairs instead of elevators.

- Go to bed at a consistent time and rest your eyes from electronic screens when you can.

- Purchase and cook healthy foods. Avoid processed food if possible.

- Wear clean clothes that fit well and make you feel good about yourself.

SOCIAL

- Take part in social activities at work and in your neighborhood.

- Take a break from social media and visit a person in real life.

- Go to parties where you can meet new people.

SPIRITUAL

- Walk barefoot in nature; do yoga, Tai Chi, or Qigong; meditate, pray, or journal.

- Spend time with other spiritual people where you feel accepted "as-is" and not judged.

- Listen to your heart, trust your intuition, and follow your dreams.

- Try to see goodness in everyone.

JOURNALING & MEDITATION

Journaling and meditation are excellent ways to practice self-care and experience peace with life. When you align with what is happening in reality, your difficulties begin to diminish. Many life problems result from a failure to respond to critical matters because of a lack of awareness, time, energy, knowledge, or resources.

When you stop fighting and arguing with life, your stress and anxiety will transform into serenity and peace. Life stops surprising you when you are conscious and aware of what is happening in the present moment. You begin to see things you used to label as "bad" as your teachers and life lessons. Journaling and meditation help answer the question, "What is life trying to teach you about yourself?"

Journaling and meditation can help you gain perspective while helping to heal your family trauma. These tools help you get in touch with reality, gain distance and space from your thoughts, and realize with gratitude how life gives you exactly what you need when you need it. Instead of listening to your inner critic, you can think about positive statements such as, "Everything is going to be alright." John Lennon said, "Everything will be okay in the end. If it's not okay, it's not the end."

Journaling and meditation can help you find inner peace by being at peace with yourself and the world around you. As you practice journaling and meditation, the power other people have over you will begin to diminish, and you will find ever-increasing peace as you become one with life in the present moment.

HOW TO JOURNAL

Since the beginning of time, humans have been recording their experiences and documenting their stories. Whether on a cave wall, papyrus, or electronically, journaling has been a part of the human experience from time immemorial. When you journal, you record what is happening in your life to process your experience, gain perspective, and understand what life is teaching you. If you need someone to talk to about your life challenges, but no one is available, your journal is always there for you. You can write down your thoughts, feelings, fears, concerns, joys, and sorrows. You can journal your hopes, dreams, prayers, wants, desires, and failures. You can even use your journal to record notes for future therapy sessions with your therapist.

TIPS FOR WRITING A JOURNAL

- Keep your journal private and in a safe place, or password protect it if it is an e-journal.
- Try to write every day.
- Write paragraphs or bullet points.
- Don't edit your journal. Let it be a stream of consciousness. It's OK to make mistakes.
- Don't worry about spelling, punctuation, or grammar.
- Write after you have had a stressful experience.
- Write if you are having difficulty solving a problem or have questions about yourself or how someone treated you.

- Just be yourself. Your audience is you. You don't have to impress anyone. Be the real you and not some cleaned-up version of yourself.

- If you don't know what to write or are staring at a blank page, write about what you think or feel. Write about what is in your heart and mind. You can always make a list of things for which you are grateful.

- Don't be afraid to ask questions in your journal, even if you have no answers or do not come to any conclusions.

- Bring your journal to your therapy session and use it as a topic for discussion.

Keep a journal to record milestones, breakthroughs, epiphanies, and discoveries about yourself. Journaling helps you keep perspective, remain present, and be mindful. Being mindful, or mindfulness, discussed in more detail in the next chapter, means being aware of what you are feeling, thinking, and experiencing in the present moment without judgment or interpretation.

How to Meditate

Like journaling, meditation can help you become centered and obtain mental perspective and clarity. In meditation, you align with what is happening within you and in the world around you. In mediation, you can learn to be still and, over time, achieve the state of no thought. When you have no thoughts, you are pure consciousness. In this state, you are your true self. In meditation, you can ask deep questions about your life and wait for answers. Meditation allows you to ground yourself in your body, connect with your spiritual nature, and stop identifying with your thoughts.

When you meditate, you are not checking out; you are checking in. To meditate, find a comfortable position for your body. Traditionally people have meditated sitting down. However, meditation can become a lifestyle. You can meditate while sitting, standing, lying down, walking in the middle of the woods, or waiting for a bus in the middle of New York City. You can meditate in your daily life, not just on your yoga mat.

Taking meditation into the hustle and bustle of your everyday life is an excellent way to take care of yourself. You can meditate on the subway or while waiting for the crosswalk light to change. You can feel the energy flowing in every part of your body, feel your breath, and be conscious of what is happening inside and around you. Through meditation, you remain connected to everything.

MANTRAS

When you first begin meditating, you will be amazed by all the noise in your mind. You can gain focus by repeating a mantra. A mantra can be a word or any group of words you repeat to center your thoughts and focus your attention. When you find your mind wandering, you can return to your mantra. You can find mantras in Buddhism, Hinduism, and the Psalms of Christianity.

Every time you find your mind wandering, repeat your mantra of choice. The positive core beliefs we will discuss in the next chapter also make excellent mantras until you find one that works best for you:

- Everything's going to be alright.
- I am more than enough.
- I am not in trouble.
- I am OK, just as I am.
- I belong.
- It's going to get easier.

- I've got this.

Meditation allows you to connect with your authentic self—an eternal expression of the one life that flows through all creation.

Meditation Techniques

- Sit in a comfortable position and set a time limit. Lie down if it makes you feel more comfortable.

- Focus your mind on your mantra and focus on your inbreath and outbreath to quiet your mind and relax. Pay attention to when you inhale and exhale. Notice how it takes longer for your body to exhale than to inhale.

- As thoughts begin to fill your mind or if you start to fall asleep, return to your mantra to help you refocus. Don't beat yourself up if you fall asleep; you need the rest.

- Focus on your body. Relax your muscles, including your abdomen and neck and the muscles around your eyes and mouth.

- Feel the life energy flowing into every part of your body. Feel the energy flowing in your toes, your hands, your chest, and every section of your body.

- Be aware of thoughts that take you back into the past or forward into the future. Stay in the present moment. Life is in the present moment. Thoughts of the past or future are only distractions from living in the moment. Past and future are only mental constructs or thoughts about the present moment.

- Your goal is to relax, clear your mind, and experience no thoughts in your consciousness. Don't judge yourself if you can't accomplish this. Always be kind and compassionate with yourself.

- Observe your thoughts as they flow in and out of your consciousness. Notice how your thoughts come and go. Because they are temporary and transitory, you don't need to identify with your thoughts or believe everything you think to be true. You are not your thoughts.

- Allow your mind and body to come to a place of rest.

- Surrender and accept what is. Be at peace with your life and the universe. Accepting what is never means accepting abusive people.

FACE YOUR PAIN

Learning to face your pain is essential to taking care of yourself. "Face your pain," "Step into your pain," and, "Turn toward your pain," are all expressions of your desire and willingness to look inward and face your trauma directly and courageously instead of blaming the outside world or running away from your problems. How do you face your pain? Rumi, a thirteenth-century Persian poet and religious leader, wrote, "The cure for pain is in the pain."

Although the outside world may be the source of your pain, the solution will always be found within yourself. Many people turn away from their pain, refuse to look inwardly, and blame the outside world. Even if you decide to walk away from toxic family members, make sure you are not running away from the pain within yourself. In most cases, your reaction to the outside world is what is causing your suffering—not the outside world itself.

Even though the outside world may have caused your trauma, you cannot simply blame the outside world for your problems.

You must look inside yourself and face your inner pain. When you deny your pain, you suffer. When you blame the outside world, you suffer. When you accept and face your pain, you find healing. If you refuse to face your trauma and it remains unhealed, you risk becoming toxic yourself. People become toxic when they take their unhealed trauma out on the people around them.

Journaling and meditation are excellent techniques for facing the pain of your past and unhealed trauma. However, sometimes in life, you need someone else's help to deal with your pain. In difficult times, such as overcoming the pain of your family trauma, you may need help from a safe and supportive friend or therapist.

How to Get Help When Needed

Even if you walk away from your toxic family, underlying issues will continue to cause you pain. This is called *trauma*. Sometimes you don't know how to look within yourself and uncover and address the underlying issues causing your pain. Some people change neighborhoods, buy new things, clean out their closets, change jobs, take vacations, change partners, or rearrange the furniture, all in an attempt to fix the outside world when the problem lies within themselves. Unhealed trauma can make you emotionally, mentally, and physically sick if you don't address it appropriately. Occasionally, it is necessary to ask for help from someone else.

There are many ways to get help when needed:

- Support groups
- Therapists, counselors, or psychiatrists
- Peer counselors
- Safe and supportive friends or relatives

Working with a therapist can help you discover what underlying issues are causing your pain and suffering. If you do not have access to a therapist, speaking to a safe, trusted, and empathetic friend can help you explore and face your trauma.

Cost can be an important factor when seeking professional help. When insurance does not cover a therapist, you can look for free services in your area from work, church, or local non-profit groups. Peer counselor sessions are often free and can be a helpful way to get the help you may need. Even if you decide not to seek help from a therapist, peer counselor, or support group, you will want to identify a friend with whom you can share your pain without judgment.

Whoever you turn to for help, make sure they are present, good listeners, and empathetic and accept you just as you are without judgment. Brené Brown, author and professor, writes, "Empathy is simply listening, holding space, withholding judgment, emotionally connecting, and communicating that incredibly healing message of 'you're not alone.'"

People who give you cliche responses that lack empathy or are judgmental are not safe and supportive. Stop sharing your life with people who say things similar to the following:

- "At least something worse didn't happen to you."
- "All families are dysfunctional; you're overreacting."
- "Are you still complaining about your childhood? Move on already."
- "Are you sure you're not remembering what happened wrong?"
- "God must be toughening you up."
- "Stop being so negative and look on the bright side of things."

- "That's the stupidest thing I've ever heard."
- "Time will heal your wounds."
- "God is making you more like Jesus."
- "You had a happy childhood."
- "You must have brought this on yourself."
- "You shouldn't feel that way."
- "You're being oversensitive."
- "You're making a mountain out of a molehill."
- "You're not over that yet?"

Anyone you share your life with must not mock, belittle, or question your recovery goals. They must accept you unconditionally and actively listen to what you are going through. Never entrust your healing to negative, critical, or judgmental people who want to change or fix you. When you share your true self with nonjudgmental people, you will learn it is OK to be yourself over time. In that safe relationship, fear, guilt, and shame diminish, and your authentic self safely emerges. Professional therapists, counselors, and psychiatrists are trained to be present, actively listen, avoid their own biases, be empathic, and accept you unconditionally, just as you are.

TOPICS FOR DISCUSSION WITH A THERAPIST

You can share anything with your therapist. If you aren't sure where to start, consider the following topics:

- Abuse
- Addiction and self-medication
- Anger and rage
- Anxiety and stress

- Body image issues
- Boundaries
- Chronic unhappiness
- Codependency and people-pleasing
- Control issues
- Depression
- Difficulty resolving conflict
- Disabilities
- Disturbing dreams
- Domestic violence
- Eating disorders
- Emotional detachment
- Failed relationships
- Fear of abandonment
- Fear of being alone
- Fear of rejection
- Fears and phobias
- Feeling numb
- Feeling overly responsible for others or feeling the need to fix others
- Grief, loss, or feeling stuck in life after losing a loved one
- High tolerance for the inappropriate behavior of others
- Homophobia, transphobia, or heterosexism
- How to be your authentic self

- Hypersensitivity to emotional invalidation
- Hypervigilance (increased state of alertness)
- Insomnia
- Isolation and loneliness
- Lacking self-acceptance
- Living in the past and future instead of the present
- Low self-esteem
- Low self-worth
- Major life change (death, job loss, relocation, etc.)
- Mental illness
- Neglect by family or partner
- Need for external validation
- Need for psychiatric medication
- Obsessive-compulsive behavior
- Overthinking, negative thinking, judgmental thinking
- Perfectionism
- Post-traumatic stress
- Romance, sexuality, sexual orientation, gender identity
- Relationship issues
- Repeating dysfunctional relationship patterns
- School and work issues
- Secrets you keep from others
- Self-acceptance
- Self-care or self-neglect

- Self-harm
- Shame and guilt
- Stress from legal or financial problems
- Stress-related illnesses
- Suicidal thoughts
- Trauma and trauma triggers
- Trust issues
- Unhealthy coping strategies
- Anything else you need to talk about

WAYS TO MAXIMIZE THE EFFECTIVENESS OF THERAPY

Below are some suggested ways to get the most out of your therapy sessions:

- Admit your faults and weaknesses honestly and openly.

- Before your therapy session, write down a list of topics you wish to discuss. After your therapy session, review what you learned, including your feelings and thoughts and what your therapist said.

- Be present. Don't get stuck in the past or future and miss what is happening in the present moment.

- Be realistic about your expectations. Healing from long-term trauma takes time!

- Be the real you, not the ideal you. Be your authentic self and not the person you think you "should" be. Don't play a role or wear a mask with your therapist.

- Be willing to discuss the most shameful thing you have ever thought or done. Discuss the guilt you may be feeling over mistakes you made in the past. Remember, no topic is off-limits.

- Be willing to explore what is causing your emotional and psychological pain.

- Be willing to look within yourself rather than blaming others or the outside world for your problems.

- Don't be afraid to disagree or challenge your therapist, but be open to learning new things and seeing different viewpoints and perspectives.

- Find another therapist if your current one isn't a good fit. If your therapist ever exhibits characteristics similar to your abusive family or is harsh, inflexible, overly strict, or judgmental, find a new one.

- Have a list of goals (what you expect to get out of therapy) and regularly evaluate those goals with your therapist.

- Journal during the week and use your journal notes as topics for your therapy sessions.

- Own up to your mistakes and your part in problematic relationships.

- Read self-help books related to the issues you are facing in therapy.

- Remember to breathe and stay in your body. Don't get stuck in your head. Feel the energy in your fingers and toes.

- Take personal responsibility for your life and mistakes.

- When your therapist says something or interrupts you, be quiet, listen, and take notes.

- There may be times when your therapist says something upsetting to you. Feel free to discuss how you feel with your therapist. If your therapist angers you, feel free to share all your feelings with them.

- If you find yourself doing all the talking, occasionally ask your therapist, "What do you think?"

QUALITIES TO LOOK FOR IN A THERAPIST

Below are qualities to look for in a therapist:

- Actively listens

- Affirming

- Compassionate

- Doesn't use the words "should" or "shouldn't"

- Doesn't tell you what to do; lets you discover your next step

- Empathetic

- Free from biases (cultural, gender, racial, religious, sexual)

- Mindful—not judgmental

- Present

- Provides a safe space

- Remembers the people and issues you've shared in past sessions

- Specializes in topics critical to your recovery (addiction, depression, LGBTQ+, PTSD, etc.)

- Unconditionally accepting

- Understanding

- Validating

HOW TO LOOK FOR A THERAPIST

Finding a therapist may take time, so be patient with the process. Here are some ways to locate a therapist:

- Ask your job if they provide counseling services.
- Ask your local church if they offer or are aware of counseling services.
- Call your health insurance provider for assistance or search your health insurance provider's online directory.
- Do an online search:
  - Psychology Today: psychologytoday.com/us/therapists
  - 211: 211.org
  - American Psychological Association: locator.apa.org
  - National Register of Health Service Psychologists: findapsychologist.org

Be open to whoever is available in your area. If you find a provider who seems like a good fit, don't take it personally if you leave a voicemail message for them and never hear back. Most mental health professionals don't have staff to answer their phones and may be too busy to take on new patients.

QUESTIONS FOR RECOVERY GOAL SETTING

Talk to your therapist about goals for your therapy and regularly discuss your progress. You can use the following questions to help you set therapy goals:

- In what areas of your life would you like to see healing?
- Is there any aspect of your life you are sick and tired of?

- Have you ever wanted to achieve something in life but couldn't?

- How would you like your life to be different after your recovery?

- What brought you into therapy in the first place?

- Where do you see your life in a year? Five years?

WHEN TO END THERAPY

Therapy can end once you have met your mental health goals and you and your therapist agree it is time to stop. Unfortunately, this isn't always the reason therapy ends. Often, your insurance company or your pocketbook will determine the length of your treatment. If your insurance company cuts you off, sometimes your therapist can contact the insurance company to discuss your progress and diagnosis and the need for additional sessions. If you cannot afford to go to a therapist weekly, consider bi-monthly or monthly if your therapist is willing.

COPING WITH DEPRESSION

Depression is a chronic mood disorder characterized by intense sadness and hopelessness.

Symptoms of depression can include the following:

- Anxiety

- Apathy

- Excessive crying

- Fatigue

- Feelings of guilt and shame
- Hopelessness
- Insomnia, restless sleep, excessive sleep
- Irritability
- Isolation
- Lack of concentration
- Lack of energy
- Lack of interest in daily activities
- Loss of pleasure in daily activities
- Low self-esteem
- Mood swings
- Overeating or undereating
- Sadness
- Self-criticism
- Weight gain or loss

As chronic depression is one of the most common symptoms of a toxic family, I deliberately included steps to overcome depression throughout this book. The following is a list of the most effective depression coping strategies:

- Practicing healthy coping behaviors such as gratitude and focusing on the positive (chapter 2)
- Using RAIN to cope with negative emotions (chapter 2)
- Walking away from people who won't stop hurting you (chapter 3)
- Hanging out with safe and supportive friends (chapter 4)

- Practicing self-care activities when you feel like you cannot differentiate between yourself and your negative emotions, thoughts, and actions, sometimes called a downward spiral of depression (chapter 5)

- Getting help when needed (chapter 5)

- Replacing your negative core beliefs with positive ones (chapter 6)

- Practicing mindfulness: Living in the present moment and accepting life on life's terms without judgment (chapter 6)

- Not focusing on your past (chapter 6)

- Not identifying with your thoughts (chapter 6)

- Not projecting your negative thoughts about the past into the future (chapter 6)

- Recognizing any cognitive errors you may have (chapter 6)

- Using RAIN to cope with negative thoughts (chapter 6)

- Expressing your authentic self at all costs and at all times in all relationships (chapter 7)

MANAGING POST-TRAUMATIC STRESS (PTSD)

Trauma is an emotional disturbance caused by a life-threatening or traumatizing event you experienced or witnessed. If the harmful effects of your trauma persist over time, you can develop post-traumatic stress or PTSD. The symptoms of PTSD are common among people who have suffered abuse and domestic violence from toxic families. With PTSD, events in the present can trigger uncontrollable thoughts and emotions that are powerfully reminiscent of your traumatic past.

PRIMARY SYMPTOMS OF PTSD

Below are possible symptoms you may experience related to PTSD. Consult a mental health professional if you experience these symptoms over an extended period (more than a month) and they interfere with your daily living. Always consult a therapist or medical professional for an accurate diagnosis and treatment of mental health symptoms.

- Avoidance (avoiding people, places, and situations that are reminiscent of the initial trauma or talking about the initial trauma)

- Flashbacks (instantly going back to the trauma in your thoughts and or emotions as if the initial trauma was happening again)

- Persistent upsetting nightmares or night terrors

- Recurring, unwanted, and intrusive memories and negative thoughts about your traumatic experience

- Intense emotional reactions to people and circumstances that remind you of the traumatic event and cause severe emotional distress or physical discomfort

ADDITIONAL SYMPTOMS OF PTSD

Symptoms of PTSD can also include the following:

- Always being on guard (hypervigilance: constantly alert to potential threats)

- Having difficulty concentrating and memory issues

- Having difficulty maintaining intimate relationships

- Being easily startled
- Having eating disorders
- Having emotional and physiological reactions such as fight or flight or physical and emotional shutdown
- Feeling emotionally numb
- Feeling detached from friends and family
- Experiencing hopelessness and depression
- Having insomnia
- Being irritable
- Experiencing isolation
- Having severe emotional responses to something in the present moment that reminds you of the initial trauma
- Abusing substances
- Having suicidal thoughts and doing self-harm

UNTREATED PTSD

Untreated PTSD can result in the following:

- A lack of support from friends and family due to difficulty maintaining relationships
- Anxiety
- Depression
- Eating disorders
- Substance abuse
- Suicidal thoughts and self-harming actions

TREATMENT FOR PTSD

See your therapist or doctor to develop a treatment plan. The treatment for PTSD can include the following:

- Therapy (primary treatment)
- Medication
- Mindfulness to cope with triggering thoughts

CHAPTER FIVE SUMMARY

The fifth step to surviving your toxic family and reclaiming your life after toxic parents is to make self-care a priority. In this chapter, we discussed self-care, journaling, meditation, and facing your pain. We also explored how to get help when needed, how to cope with depression, and how to manage PTSD. In chapter 6, we will discuss how to stop toxic thinking.

CHAPTER 6

— ❧ —

STOP TOXIC THINKING

I think, therefore I am not here.
—THICH NHAT HANH

The sixth step to surviving your toxic family & reclaiming your life after toxic parents is to stop toxic thinking.

Now that you've learned how to cope with your family, set boundaries, walk away if necessary, and take care of yourself, it is time to stop those unwanted and unhelpful thoughts that fill your mind. The information in this chapter will assist you in transforming negative thought patterns into peaceful ones. A calm mind is essential for overcoming your toxic family.

In this chapter, we will explore the following:

1. Journal Part VI: Rock Bottom

2. 5 Types of Toxic Thinking

3. Avoiding Stress-Inducing Thoughts

4. Cognitive Errors, Negative Core Beliefs & Your Inner Critic

5. Being Present & Mindfulness to Eliminate Toxic Thinking

6. Journaling & Meditation to Observe Your Thoughts

7. Observing Your Thoughts with RAIN

JOURNAL PART VI: ROCK BOTTOM

My parents were the voice of my inner critic. Even though they lived 1,200 miles away, I still argued with them daily in my head. They taught me how to judge, criticize, loathe myself, and blame others. Even after I moved to California and had little or no contact with my parents, I spent decades trying to prove to them I was a valuable human being.

Alcohol always quieted my inner critic and shut down the part of my brain that worried and obsessed over things. Once I became sober, I became aware of every problem I ever had, and my mind became filled with toxic thinking. Negative and fearful thoughts once again filled my mind. I couldn't turn my brain off. I started worrying about my reputation at the university and projected all my worst-case scenarios into the future. Suddenly, losing my job and going bankrupt became a real possibility. Without any savings to speak of, I feared I would end up homeless and on the street.

Because my boss at the university told me I had to deal with my alcohol abuse if I wanted to keep my job, I entered my first rehab program at a hospital in Culver City, California. After years of soothing my pain and self-medicating my childhood trauma with alcohol, I was ready to face reality and take a hard look at my life. The rehab was a day program, permitting me to go home at night, which was risky in early sobriety. After so many years of using alcohol to fall asleep every night, my first night back home was challenging. I wondered if I would ever fall asleep again or learn to cope with my life without alcohol.

Once I completed the two-week rehab program in Culver City, the college dean called me into another meeting to discuss my future employment. I feared the worst and spent hours worrying beforehand, predicting the worst-case scenario, and practicing a speech I would give in my defense: "I had a problem with alcohol, but that's all behind me now. I'm 100 percent ready to get back to work, take care of myself, and make the success of the university my first priority."

I was surprised to learn the dean was promoting me to director of communications, not firing me. I was so lost in my thoughts that it took me several minutes to figure out what was happening. She had to repeat herself about the new job title and promotion before I finally got it. I think that's what Thich Nhat Hanh meant when he said, "I think, therefore I am not here."

Once sober and working hard in my new position, I filled my free time attending AA meetings near my home in Long Beach, California. As I became more clear-headed, I realized I wanted to get off the antidepressants I had been taking for nearly twenty years. In 2009, I met with my psychiatrist, who agreed I could stop taking the antidepressants. I asked him if I needed to taper off the medication gradually, and he told me to stop taking them all at once—a colossal mistake.

Almost immediately after stopping the antidepressants, I started to lose touch with reality. I began hearing voices and experiencing hallucinations. I began to misinterpret what was happening around me. I remember walking by a neighboring apartment and hearing a baby cry. In my mind, I thought it was my mother crying 1,200 miles away, as she was still dealing with my father's domestic violence.

A few weeks later, I thought swimming naked in the Long Beach harbor on a sunny day sounded like a really good idea. I walked to the beach, stripped off my clothes, and swam naked in the warm Pacific Ocean. Within a few minutes, a police car, a lifeguard Jeep, and an ambulance appeared on the service road near where I was swimming.

The officers told me to come out of the water and asked me where my clothes were, but I couldn't remember where I had left them. They put a yellow plastic blanket around me. I thought one of the emergency medical technicians looked like Jesus and told him so. It was apparent by my behavior that instead of arresting me for public indecency, they needed to take me to the psychiatric ward of a nearby hospital for evaluation. This was psychiatric hospital #1. They put me on a 5150 hold and detained me for seventy-two hours while they assessed my mental health condition. They believed I was a danger to myself and others.

Sitting in the psychiatric ward, I felt as if my body was beginning to shut down. They put me in one of those padded rooms with some other men for hours, and all I wanted to do was get out. I was still wearing the yellow plastic blanket the police gave me because I had lost my clothes at the beach. Some of the men in the psych ward seemed dangerous, and I felt like I was unsafe and didn't belong. A few hours later, they moved me to another hospital floor and gave me a bed in a room with four other men in a locked unit.

One of my roommates kept threatening me and would wake me up in the middle of the night and say he was going to beat me up, but he never did. I was hypervigilant the whole time I was there. Eventually, they found some clothes from the lost and found, but the jeans they gave me were several sizes too small. I walked around with my pants half open for the entire week since I couldn't button them all the way. To cover and hide my exposed body, I stretched and pulled down the T-shirt they gave me that was too small.

The first thing I did was call my parents to tell them where I was. I called them several times that week, hoping they would come and get me or convince the doctors to let me out. After a few days, I tried calling again and got a recording that I had reached a number that had been disconnected. I called the operator, who confirmed that the recording was correct. When I asked the operator if my parents had a new number, he told me their new number was unlisted.

The entire time I was in the hospital suffering from a mental breakdown, I was out of touch with my family. Years later, my mom told me my dad was so irritated by my disturbing phone calls and their effect on my mom that he told her to unlist their phone number. My feelings of being alone in the world, unsafe, and not belonging in the psych ward grew with each passing day. Seven days later, I was released from the hospital, given a bus token home, and found my way back to my apartment.

A few weeks later, I was still hallucinating and hearing voices. I was too out of it to schedule an appointment with my psychiatrist. Instead, I drove my car to the Belmont Shore area of Long Beach. I left my wallet, phone, and keys on the porch of a house near where I parked. I think I was trying to rid myself of all my earthly possessions. I walked to the beach, and this time I kept my clothes on and sat down on the sand. A helicopter flew past me, circled, and hovered directly above me. Hallucinating, I thought my psychiatrist was in the helicopter spying on me. I lay back in the warm sand and fell asleep.

I awoke to find the helicopter gone. I looked for my car, keys, phone, and wallet, but I couldn't remember where I had left them. I walked several miles back to my apartment, and without my keys, I had to break in. I couldn't lock my front door for several months because I had broken the lock and had no keys. I didn't have the sense at the time to call the landlord and have the lock fixed or the keys replaced.

I eventually got up the nerve to call my psychiatrist. I bought a disposable phone at the local 7-Eleven store and told my psychiatrist I was hallucinating. He asked me if I could find my way to his office, and I thought I could. When I got to his office, he immediately put me on another 5150 hold and admitted me to the psychiatric hospital where he served as medical director. This was psychiatric hospital #2. I didn't see him for a few days but kept asking the nurses if I could see my doctor. Eventually, he showed up and met with me. I asked him what was wrong with me. He said two words: "Psychotic break," got up, and left the room.

I spent the next three years in and out of psychiatric hospitals while my brain adapted to life without alcohol and antidepressants. Two times I voluntarily admitted myself to the psych ward at Long Beach's Community Hospital. That was psychiatric hospital #3. They had the best food. The hospital which helped me the most was Las Encinas Hospital in Pasadena, California, under the direction of Dr. Drew Pinsky, known for his TV show *Celebrity Rehab*. I went there to get into their rehab program, but after a few days, they moved me into their psych ward for an evaluation. That was psychiatric hospital #4.

After a few days in the psychiatric section, they let me out and allowed me to re-enter the rehab program. Bob Forrest led my favorite support group at Las Encinas. He was a recovered drug addict and former lead singer of the band Thelonious Monster. A documentary was made about his life called *Bob and the Monster* in 2011.

After three years of not drinking and adjusting to life without antidepressants, I stopped hearing voices and hallucinating. I slowly started to pull my life back together. I never again suffered from any symptoms similar to those I experienced during my mental breakdown. Needless to say, all of the time spent in psych wards caused me to lose my lucrative job at the university. I can't blame them for not keeping my job open indefinitely.

Since I was no longer employed, I eventually ran out of money. I got a job as a part-time teller at a local bank and attended AA meetings in the afternoon and on weekends. My favorite AA meeting was near the canals in Naples, California, next to Long Beach. I began to notice this handsome Latino who looked like a movie star with his striking good looks and perfect smile. He always shared with the group how God was the source of his sobriety, which impressed me to no end. The moment I first laid eyes on him, it was love at first sight.

I summoned the courage to ask him if he wanted to go out and grab a cup of coffee after the meeting. He said, "No, but do you want to pray?"

I said, "Sure!"

We prayed for about fifteen minutes in his car and exchanged phone numbers. The two of us bonded quickly, attended AA meetings, and began going to church together at Calvary Chapel in Costa Mesa. Eventually, we shared an apartment and were in a relationship that started as a friendship and became much more after six years. I felt like all my dreams came true the day he told me he wanted to marry me someday.

All my life, I had closed my heart to people because of my family wounds. I felt like it was safe to be myself and vulnerable with him. I never felt judged for being my authentic self. He was the first person to love the real me without conditions. Over time, he broke through the wounds and scars of my childhood abuse and opened my heart. For the first time since I was a small child, I felt love at the core of my being. He was the love of my life.

He always brought out the best in me and made me feel more like myself. He helped my authentic life to shine through me in ways I had never experienced before. Because I am an introvert, I find most people draining. When I was with him, I never felt like I needed to take a break or recharge my batteries. He didn't complete me but brought out the best in me. For six years, we spent practically every second of every hour of every day together, which was never enough.

My deepest regret was that we didn't live happily ever after. Shortly after telling me he wanted to marry me, he died in a tragic accident, and my heart shattered. To add tragedy to tragedy, within months, both of my parents died as well. I had to hit rock bottom before saying, "I surrender."

STOP TOXIC THINKING

5 TYPES OF TOXIC THINKING

How your family treated you and what they said about you affected your thoughts about yourself, others, and the world around you. Your inner critic developed as a result of the negative, judgmental, shameful, and critical things they told you about yourself. A negative inner critic misinterprets who you are and what is happening in the world around you. Your inner critic is most likely your toxic parent's voice in your head.

If you are like me, your inner voice may be so critical of you that you experience self-hatred and self-loathing, the terms psychologists use to describe intense self-criticism. For me, self-loathing is the feeling that I've done something wrong, I'm not good enough, I'm in trouble, I'm defective, and I don't belong anywhere. Once I learned to recognize these intensely self-critical thoughts, I became free of them. I also memorized positive core beliefs about myself.

To experience a peaceful mind, you must be at peace with yourself, the people around you, and the conditions and circumstances of your life. If you silence your inner critic but are constantly at war with the external world, you will never find peace.

Your family may have taught you one or more of the five types of toxic thinking:

1. Cynical hostility
2. Judgmentalism
3. Limiting beliefs
4. Negative rumination
5. Overthinking

1. Cynical Hostility

Cynical hostility, or *cynicism*, is where you assume the worst intentions of those around you. Rather than looking for the good in people, you project your own anger, pain, and weaknesses onto others. Your parents taught you how to see the worst in yourself and others. The harm caused by this worldview can lead to stress and physical illnesses such as heart conditions.

2. Judgmentalism

Judgmentalism is when you disapprove, condemn, find fault, and judge people and circumstances. Carl Yung said, "Everything that irritates us about others can lead us to an understanding of ourselves." People who habitually judge and shame others are often unconsciously conflicted about their own imperfections. Judgmentalism can cause stress and high blood pressure and weakens your immune system.

3. LIMITING BELIEFS

Limiting beliefs are ways of thinking about yourself or how the world works that prevent you from taking action. These beliefs are fundamentally fear based and are often false. You believe something to be absolutely true about the world or yourself, which limits your life options based on your erroneous beliefs. For example, you might think, "I'm not good enough," which you learned from your toxic family members. Limiting beliefs restrict your ability to make healthy decisions and take healthy risks, and hinder your personal development.

Limiting beliefs can paralyze you as well. You may believe you don't have enough money to get better housing or you don't have the skills to get a better job. You may not approach someone you are attracted to because of your limiting belief that you are unlovable or unattractive. You may never fulfill your dreams because of some limiting belief about yourself or life, which prevents you from taking action. Limiting beliefs prevent you from living your best life.

4. NEGATIVE RUMINATION

Negative rumination is a negative thought pattern where you replay the same negative thoughts over and over in your mind like a broken record. Your negative rumination is often compulsive, and unwanted and feels out of your control. These repetitive negative thoughts get stuck in your head, and you may spend hours repeating them. Negative rumination and other types of toxic thinking stem from the trauma you experienced in your dysfunctional family as well as behaviors your family taught you. Negative ruminations can cause anxiety and often lead to hopelessness and depression when you project your worst-case scenarios into the future.

5. OVERTHINKING

Overthinking occurs when you get stuck in a pattern of unproductive thought. When you overthink, it's like trying to solve a puzzle with no solution. Or you may already have a solution to the life puzzle, but you second-guess your conclusion and continue to obsess over the question. People who overthink often need help getting out of the research phase of decision-making. Writers who overthink get stuck in the editing process. Overthinking is almost always related to thoughts of the past or the future. Remaining in the present moment in your thoughts can reduce and eliminate overthinking. Overthinking is about doubting yourself and your words, actions, and decisions, and unproductively replaying your mistakes and the behavior of others over and over in your mind. Overthinking can cause fatigue, headaches, insomnia, and nausea. Meditation is an excellent cure for overthinking.

AVOIDING STRESS-INDUCING THOUGHTS

In addition to being aware of the five types of toxic thinking, you can dramatically reduce your stress, anxiety, and negative thinking based on the thoughts you choose to think. To reduce your stress, you can avoid the following types of stress-inducing thoughts:

1. Things you cannot control
2. Other people's business and God's business
3. Past and future

1. THINGS YOU CANNOT CONTROL

Epictetus, a second-century philosopher, wrote, "There is only one way to happiness and that is to cease worrying about things which are beyond the power of our will." To significantly reduce stress and anxiety, you can limit the time you spend negatively thinking about things beyond your control. Misunderstanding your level of control over life is a source of incredible frustration, leading to all sorts of negative emotions such as anger, anxiety, guilt, and shame. Despite what you might think, you do not have much control over your own life. The sooner you can be at peace with this fact, the sooner you will experience a greater serenity. You do not control your breath, heartbeat, or when you will die. You have no control over the behavior of others or what happens in life. Whenever you try to control things out of your control, you experience negative and critical thoughts about how people and the world don't do what you want. A good question to ask yourself might be, "Why am I trying to control life?" or, "Why am I trying to control other people?" Perhaps your search for control has to do with a controlling parent or is an unconscious attempt to heal the out-of-control feelings you felt living in your toxic family. You only have the power to change yourself and how you react to life. Spending time worrying about things out of your control is a poor use of your time and causes stress, anxiety, and suffering.

2. OTHER PEOPLE'S BUSINESS & GOD'S BUSINESS

With her ground-breaking self-inquiry method, *The Work*, author and teacher Byron Katie developed another way to think about letting go of what you cannot control. One of her fundamental principles is, "There are only three kinds of business in the universe: mine, yours, and God's." One of the questions she challenges you to ask yourself is, "Whose business are you in?" When you worry about other people's actions, thoughts, or words, you are in someone else's business. You are in God's business when you begin worrying about natural disasters or what might happen in the future. Whenever you encounter a roadblock in life or come up against something you cannot change, you are either in God's business or somebody else's business.

If you want to eliminate your stress and anxiety, you must get back into your own business and surrender to what you cannot control. Knowing what you can change and what you cannot is part of being at peace with life. You mimic your family's dysfunctional and unhealthy behavior when you try to manipulate and control other people, conditions, or circumstances.

To avoid suffering in life, you must accept yourself and everything that is out of your control. The only other option is non-acceptance. When you worry about things outside your control, you always experience stress and suffering. Accepting what is out of your control does not mean tolerating mistreatment or abuse from others. Never tolerate abuse or mistreatment.

3. PAST & FUTURE

Fear only exists in the future; guilt and shame only exist in the past. Spending time thinking about the past or the future is a common type of stress-producing thought. Because past and future events are entirely out of your control, you experience stress and suffering whenever you think negatively about these time constructs.

Most of us have everything we need in the present moment. Your disturbing thoughts are almost always about what already happened or about what you predict will happen. You tell yourself stories about what happened in the past and what terrible things might occur in the future. It is best to stay in the present moment, avoid making up stories (thoughts about what happened or may happen to us), and stick to the facts. If you stop worrying about the past, future, or things out of your control, you will experience less stress, anxiety, and suffering. Most of life's problems are in the past or future, not in the present moment.

In addition to stress-inducing thoughts, cognitive errors, and negative core beliefs are also significant causes of stress, anxiety, and suffering. These are the tools your inner critic uses to beat you up and misinterpret life.

COGNITIVE ERRORS, NEGATIVE CORE BELIEFS & YOUR INNER CRITIC

Your inner critic continuously reminds you of the same negative beliefs about yourself and gets stuck in the same repetitive, unwanted negative thinking patterns. Your inner critic is the source of your cognitive errors and negative core beliefs about yourself.

Cognitive errors are thinking patterns that distort your perceptions of reality, such as catastrophizing or all-or-nothing thinking. Negative core beliefs are those negative self-loathing thoughts you have about yourself, such as, "I am not good enough," or, "I am unlovable." Negative core beliefs and cognitive errors are the tools your inner critic uses to produce a toxic mind and unhealthy thinking.

Your toxic thinking patterns originate from your toxic family and the trauma they caused you. Your inner critic is your voice of self-criticism and may mimic what you heard from parents, a teacher, a coach, or a boss who criticized you and diminished your self-esteem. If you grew up in a toxic family, there is a good chance your parent is your inner critic, continually voicing unhealthy ways of thinking about yourself and the world. There is no present-moment basis for toxic thinking other than triggers from your past or fear about the future. Your criticisms of yourself and misinterpretations of the world around you are rooted in your toxic family trauma rather than the present moment.

Learning about the cognitive errors you make and the negative core beliefs you believe about yourself can help you quiet your inner critic and identify your unhealthy ways of thinking. Your therapist can also help you identify any negative core beliefs and cognitive errors that may be causing you suffering.

COGNITIVE ERRORS

Cognitive errors, which are dysfunctional ways of thinking, are also known as *cognitive distortions* or *thinking errors*. Because unhealthy thinking was a daily occurrence in your toxic family, their distorted reactions to the world became normative behavior. If you challenged their faulty thinking, your parents most likely challenged you, shamed you, or became angry. You had to adopt their dysfunctional ways of thinking to survive in your toxic family.

TYPES OF COGNITIVE ERRORS

Here are the different types of cognitive errors you may have experienced:

ALL OR NOTHING THINKING

All-or-nothing thinking, sometimes called *black-and-white thinking*, refers to your tendency to view life in extremes rather than as a continuum. You fail to see shades of gray. Life is either one of two extremes: positive or negative, good or bad. In this false dichotomy, you lose the nuances of reality. Truth always lies somewhere in the middle. This way of thinking both idealizes and devalues life.

Perceiving life and others as one of two extremes is inaccurate and minimizing. A "bad" situation, person, or condition might contain "good" elements and, in reality, are a combination of both. Examples of all-or-nothing thinking might be as follows: "Everything always goes wrong in my life; nothing ever goes right," "I'm always going to be sick; I'm never going to get well," and, "My life will never be successful; I'm a total failure."

ALWAYS BEING RIGHT

Always being right is a cognitive error when you believe your viewpoints are not opinions but absolute facts of life and you try to convince everyone you are correct and they "should" adopt your point of view. If you are always right, then everyone else is always wrong, which leaves no room for alternative viewpoints. You open up your life to more possibilities when you can imagine that other viewpoints are possible and equally valid.

BLAMING

Blaming is the opposite of personalization. You refuse to accept your part in a given situation and instead blame others and outside circumstances for your shortcomings. You project your failures, weaknesses, and unhealed pain onto others. You mistakenly believe your problems are caused by something outside of yourself. Blaming is a defense mechanism preventing you from facing the truth about yourself and reality. Life's problems are never solved by blaming something or someone outside of yourself. Blame, in itself, is not a helpful mental exercise. Blaming someone or something never leads to a solution; instead, it causes you to exert negative mental and emotional energy with no positive results.

CATASTROPHIZING

Catastrophizing is when you assume the worst possible outcome for the future. The fear of a catastrophic future is often rooted in your traumatic and painful past, which you anticipate will repeat itself. Fear can only exist in thoughts about the future. Eliminate thoughts of the future, and you will eliminate fear. Almost always, everything is OK in the present moment. While anxiety can have some protective benefits, catastrophizing has no value, and the terrible thing you predict seldom occurs. When you project your fears into the future, you experience anxiety, stress, hopelessness, and depression.

COMPARING

The cognitive error of *comparison* is when you judge yourself or others as inferior or superior without considering strengths and weaknesses. A common comparison error is when you compare someone's strengths to your weaknesses. For example, I might think, "I'm not as good-looking as Brad Pitt." Comparison can also be a form of judgmentalism when applied to others. You might think, "She is not as good a Christian as I am," which is fundamentally antithetical to the teachings of Christianity. Comparing your weaknesses to other people's strengths can result in unhappiness and low self-esteem. When you project your shortcomings into the future, comparison can lead to hopelessness and depression. Sensei Ogui wrote, "A flower does not think of competing to the flower next to it. It just blooms."

DISCOUNTING THE POSITIVE

Discounting the positive occurs when you reject the positive because, for some reason, it doesn't count. For example, you might discount a promotion at work with the thought, "I just got lucky," when in reality, you were the most qualified. You overlook positive things happening to you based on luck or being in the right place at the right time without considering your positive qualities and achievements. Discounting the positives in life negatively impacts your self-esteem and robs you of joy.

EMOTIONAL REASONING

Emotional reasoning is interpreting your present reality based on how you feel. For example, you may feel like you are in trouble and therefore believe you are in trouble. You may feel scared and therefore think you are in danger. You may feel guilty, so you must have done something wrong. When you use emotional reasoning, you allow your emotions to rule your rational thoughts and intellect. Emotional reasoning makes you believe something is true despite the lack of evidence or evidence to the contrary. Your ability to see reality as it is and think about your life accurately improves when you learn how to process your negative emotions and not allow them to govern or guide you. Because of your toxic family experience, your feelings do not always accurately represent what is happening to you in reality.

LABELING

When you label a person or a situation, you make judgments about their value based on one descriptor. For example, you may label someone as "stupid" or "lazy." These labels reduce and minimize others to one characteristic while ignoring the complexity of their whole person. Labels are often projections of your own biases, fears, prejudices, and insecurities. When you minimize people with labels, you reduce their value and identity to one flaw or weakness, often the same flaw or weakness you experience yourself. It is easy to identify in others what we know to be true about ourselves.

MAGNIFICATION OR MINIMIZATION

Magnification and *minimization* are cognitive errors distorting reality by wrongly evaluating the importance of a situation or problem. Magnification is blowing things out of proportion. Minimization is diminishing the importance of something. In magnification, you make a mountain out of a molehill. In minimization, you make a molehill out of a mountain.

MIND-READING

Mind-reading is knowing with total certainty how other people think and feel about you or a particular situation. Without asking questions or confirming with the other person, you assume you accurately know someone else's thoughts, judgments, and intentions. In mind-reading, you draw conclusions without adequate evidence. Mind-reading is often based not on reality but on judgments, biases, and projections of your own fears and weaknesses onto others.

OVERGENERALIZATION

Overgeneralization is when you make a conclusion based on one outcome or piece of evidence. If something "bad" happens once, you assume it will occur in the same manner every time. One instance becomes an overall pattern. One single occurrence becomes a rule that applies the same way to every occasion. When you use words like "always" or "never," you are often overgeneralizing. When "bad" things happen once, the chances of that same thing happening in precisely the same manner is extremely unlikely. When you overgeneralize, you believe this one "bad" experience is how the world always works. For example, if your first boyfriend broke your heart, you may overgeneralize that all boyfriends will always break your heart.

PERSONALIZATION

Personalization is the belief that you are the reason why people behave as they do. Most people's behavior has nothing to do with you but reflects their own internal world, upbringing, thinking, fears, struggles, and trauma. When you personalize, you believe you are the cause of something which has nothing to do with you. For example, if the grocery store cashier is rude to you, you might personalize the encounter and assume they were rude because of something you did or because of who you are. However, chances are, their behavior has absolutely nothing to do with you. Personalization can stem from an inaccurate and unconscious belief that a person is the center of the universe and that the purpose of all life centers around them. When, in reality, we are all part of a complex whole, and what happens in life is seldom about us.

SHOULD & SHOULD-NOT STATEMENTS

Should and should-not statements (should, ought, must, need to) are rules you impose on others because you believe they are universal and everyone must follow them, or they will suffer negative consequences. Should or should-not statements about the past can cause guilt and shame in others; using should or should-not statements in the future is a subtle way to control and manipulate others. Whenever people in your life use words like should, should not, ought, must, or need to, it might be a sign they do not accept you for who you are and are trying to control you.

Negative Effects of Cognitive Errors

Cognitive errors can negatively impact your life in the following ways:

- Cognitive errors focused on you can lower your self-esteem and cause anxiety, depression, guilt, and shame.

- Cognitive errors focused on others can result in anger, bitterness, illusory feelings of superiority, and resentment.

- Cognitive errors about the past and future can lead to anxiety, helplessness, hopelessness, depression, and self-defeating thoughts and behaviors.

Cognitive errors cause you to see problems where there are none, which hinders human interactions, negatively misinterprets the world, and predicts catastrophic outcomes when everything is fine.

Negative Core Beliefs

Core beliefs are beliefs you have about yourself and how the world works. *Negative core beliefs* always have to do with some variation of feeling worthless, unlovable, or helpless, which you learned from your toxic family. Your inner critic uses your parents' harmful words to condemn you. These negative core beliefs determine your expectations of life, how you react to difficult circumstances, and how you interpret the behavior of others and are powerful beliefs you have about yourself. As with limiting beliefs, negative core beliefs prevent you from living your best life.

Here are some common examples of negative core beliefs learned in childhood from your toxic family:

- I am *not* OK just as I am.

- I am a failure.

- I am a terrible person.

- I am damaged.

- I am helpless.

- I am not good.

- I am shameful.

- I am ugly.

- I am unlovable.

- I am weak.

- I am worthless.

- I cannot trust myself.

- I cannot trust my intuition.

- I cannot trust my judgment.

- I don't belong.

These negative core beliefs can act like a mantra in meditation, where you negatively ruminate about yourself for an extended period, losing your serenity and damaging your sense of well-being. Every negative core belief you have about yourself can become a positive core belief by reversing them into a statement that better describes who you are and how valuable you are as a human being.

Positive Core Beliefs to Quiet Your Inner Critic

Positive core beliefs are healthy thoughts about who you are—your authentic self. Replacing negative core beliefs with positive ones can promote happiness, joy, peace, and well-being. You can memorize them and remind yourself of these positive core beliefs by setting daily reminders on your electronic calendar, posting them on your refrigerator, saying them to yourself as affirmations, or using them as mantras in meditation.

Examples of positive core beliefs are as follows:

- I am OK just as I am.
- Everything's going to be alright.
- I am a unique and precious person.
- I am more than enough.
- I am lovable just as I am and worthy of self-love.
- I am not in trouble.
- I am strong.
- I am successful.
- I belong.
- I can be OK even if everyone around me isn't.
- I can help myself.
- I can trust myself.
- I can trust my judgment.
- I can trust my intuition.
- I have everything I need for now.
- I have what it takes.
- I have value.
- It's going to get easier.
- I've got this.

Changing your core beliefs is an example of how you can rewire your brain from being negative and judgmental to being positive and healthy. When you believe the truth about yourself, your expectation of how life will treat you will also change for the positive. Your interpretations of how people treat you will also improve. Changing your core beliefs will change the negative voice in your head and silence your inner critic.

When faced with a stressful situation, the person who thinks, "I am enough," will have a different life experience than the person who thinks, "I am worthless." Changing your core beliefs about who you are can take anywhere from a month to several months. It takes time to change behavior and create a new habit. The more you think about and meditate on positive beliefs about yourself, the healthier your thinking will become.

BEING PRESENT & MINDFULNESS TO ELIMINATE TOXIC THINKING

Another technique for eliminating unhealthy, judgmental, and negative thinking is being present and mindful. *Being present* means living in the present moment rather than in the past or the future. But being present isn't just about time. In mindfulness, being present means living in the moment and accepting everything happening now without judgment: yourself, people, circumstances, and conditions. Anytime you argue with, fight, or resist the present moment (yourself, people, circumstances, conditions), you suffer. If you are experiencing stress, you can ask yourself, "What am I resisting or judging in the present moment?"

In mindfulness, you are aware of your thoughts, emotions, and body in the present moment and view the world around you with compassion and acceptance. Mindfulness is living in the present moment and accepting life on life's terms without judgment. When you live in the present moment, mindfully accept life without judgment, and view yourself and the world with compassion, your toxic thinking diminishes significantly.

The judgments you make about yourself, others, circumstances, and conditions in the present moment are the primary source of your stress and suffering. Epictetus wrote in the second century, "We are not disturbed by what happens to us, but by our thoughts about what happens to us." Most of the suffering in life is caused by thoughts, particularly judgments about other people, ourselves, and how the world is treating us. If you want to eliminate toxic thinking and suffering in life, accept what is happening in reality. What choice do you have but to accept reality?

JOURNALING & MEDITATION TO OBSERVE YOUR THOUGHTS

The practice of journaling and meditating allows you to gain space, perspective, and distance between yourself and what you are thinking. Being able to distinguish between your thoughts and your identity is called *observing your thoughts*. You are not your thoughts. Many people confuse their identity with what they think. However, your thoughts are separate from who you are. Thoughts say nothing about your identity. Thoughts occur in your brain in what is called your *consciousness*. You are the consciousness in which the thoughts are occurring. Thoughts come and go, but you remain as consciousness. Journaling and meditation can help you see this separation between your thoughts and your consciousness. When you begin to see the separation between yourself from your thoughts, this distance allows you to gain a proper perspective on reality. When you get too close to your thoughts, especially negative ones, you lose perspective and forget who you are. In the same way, you can learn to separate your identity from your emotions, reactions, and viewpoints. Learning not to identify with your thoughts is a powerful way to overcome toxic thinking.

If you are interested in learning more about not identifying with your thoughts, I highly recommend the following book:

- *The Power of Now*, Eckhart Tolle

OBSERVING YOUR THOUGHTS WITH RAIN

Using the RAIN tool we discussed in chapter 2, you can practice mindfulness and eliminate negative thinking by actively observing and not identifying with your thoughts, particularly negative ones.

R: Recognize

A: Allow

I: Investigate

N: No Identification

RECOGNIZE

The first step of recognition is to observe the negative thought. You can observe the thought as if from a distance. You can see the space between you and your thoughts. You can see thoughts are not who you are. Thoughts, like feelings, come and go in your consciousness.

ALLOW

Once you have recognized the negative thought is not you, you can allow it to be. You don't have to beat yourself up or judge yourself for having the thought. The thought has nothing to do with your identity; it is a temporary form that comes and goes.

INVESTIGATE

When you investigate, you do not judge your thoughts but are curious. You ask yourself questions about the thought:

- Is this negative thought a cognitive error?
- Is this negative thought a negative core belief?
- Is this thought even true?
- Is the opposite of the thought also true or more true?
- Is there another viewpoint from which I can view this experience?

NO IDENTIFICATION

Finally, thoughts have nothing to do with your identity. You may have heard it said, "You are what you think." This is incorrect. Who you are is much more profound than the fleeting thoughts that pass through your mind. Thoughts are separate from your identity and who you are. You are the consciousness that observes the temporary thoughts. You are the space in which the thoughts happen.

CHAPTER SIX SUMMARY

The sixth step to surviving your toxic family & reclaiming your life after toxic parents is to stop toxic thinking. In this chapter, we explored types of toxic thinking, stress-inducing thoughts, and how to manage the cognitive errors and core beliefs of your inner critic. We discussed being present and mindful to stop toxic thinking, journaling, meditation, and RAIN to observe your thoughts instead of being them. In chapter 7, we will discuss how to live your authentic life.

CHAPTER 7

— ❧ —

LIVE YOUR AUTHENTIC LIFE

The privilege of a lifetime is to become who
you truly are.

—CARL YUNG

**The seventh step to surviving your toxic family & reclaiming
your life after toxic parents is to be your authentic self
at all costs, at all times, and in all relationships.**

Now that you have learned you can eliminate toxic thinking
and observe your thoughts rather than be them, it's time to
let go of the past and live your authentic life in the present
moment. Don't let anyone stop you from being your authentic and
best self, and stay away from people who won't stop screwing with
your life.

In this chapter, we will explore the following:

1. Journal Part VII: Finding My Authentic Life

2. Forgive, Move On & Let Go

3. Your Toxic Family Isn't Your Fault

4. Live Your Authentic Life

JOURNAL PART VII: FINDING MY AUTHENTIC LIFE

I was devastated when the love of my life died tragically in a terrible accident after six years together. I never thought I would recover from such a significant loss, and part of me never will. I thought my toxic family had already broken my heart, but the news of his death broke my heart into a million pieces. I cried endless tears until there were none left to cry. Only raw pain and an emptiness remained. I thought we would spend the rest of our lives together, but life had a different plan.

Shortly after he passed away, my father died suddenly from undiagnosed cancer. Four months later, I received a call from my mother informing me she had terminal cancer and had only months to live. She wanted to die peacefully at home in hospice. Her suffering caused me a great deal of emotional grief and pain. I spoke to her every day those past few months and made sure she always had a dozen fresh roses in her bedroom. She died four months later.

I regret I never made peace with my father while he was alive. Despite his repeated attempts to ask for forgiveness over the phone in his last years, I refused to accept his apology. Before he died, I believed my dad had given up his right to be my father. Once he passed away, everything felt different, and I wished we had talked in healing ways about our differences.

I think the death of a loved one challenges our illusory belief that we are gods. Our subconscious believes we are the center of the universe, can control life, and will never die. If we are paying attention, we will soon learn that life is a journey of loss. Everything in life is temporary. We are born into this world with nothing. We spend our lives attaching to people and things, eventually losing them all. Only our authentic self remains —an eternal expression of the one life that flows through all creation.

160

As if the universe wanted to wake me up, the Covid-19 pandemic struck immediately after these three sudden deaths. In December 2019, we started to hear rumors of an ominously looming global pandemic. My boss at the corporate offices of the bank I worked for in Seal Beach, California, would give us daily reports and predictions about how severe the pandemic would be. She was getting her information from discussion groups online. At first, my coworkers and I thought she was overreacting to the pandemic when she started predicting over a million deaths worldwide, a significant blow to the world's economy, and how Covid would push our healthcare system to the brink.

I soon realized that everything my boss told us about the pandemic was beginning to happen. Over the weekend, I took a long drive along the Pacific Coast Highway between Malibu and Point Magu. You've seen this road a thousand times in car commercials and films. I had the windows down and was listening full blast to a cover of Radiohead's song "Creep." I began to wonder, what am I doing with my life? Who am I? Who is my family? Where do I belong? That was the day I surrendered to life and began to wake up to discover my true self.

I pulled over to the side of the road and began to cry. Deep convulsive sobs thrust my chest outward as I tried hard to breathe. I didn't feel like I belonged anywhere, not in Los Angeles, not in what was left of my family, and not in my hometown Seattle. At that moment, I realized I wasn't looking for a place to belong—I was looking for myself.

That weekend, I decided to move back to the Pacific Northwest, where I had grown up and gone to college. I felt a strong desire to get extensive therapy and renew relationships with my extended family, who I hoped would also be there for me as a support system. Additionally, I wanted to document my recovery process, which ultimately became this book.

I started what turned out to be a three-year journey to find my authentic self. I bought a small home sight unseen on the internet in Port Townsend, Washington. I had heard Frank Herbert wrote the third Dune book there, which I felt was a good omen. I also heard rumors Port Townsend had a powerful spiritual energy vortex. Port Townsend sounded like the perfect place to get professional help and write a book.

I packed my few possessions into a U-Haul and moved to my new home at the end of the Olympic Peninsula in Washington state. Once I settled in, I immediately began to search for two things: (1) a church and (2) a therapist. All the local churches were closed during the pandemic, but one near my house had a men's Bible study meeting in person.

After examining their website, it was clear that the beliefs of their faith were more in line with my mother's religious views than mine. I could tell from the language on their website that I would not be welcome at this church. Although I wanted the opportunity to study the Bible and worship with other Christians, I knew this church was not a good fit and would not accept me as the person God created me to be. I decided to put finding a church home on hold during the height of the pandemic and temporarily attended a small Catholic church in a nearby town.

Looking for a therapist was very time-consuming and frustrating during the pandemic. I called and emailed about fifteen counselors within fifty miles and got no response. Initially, I wanted a Christian therapist but decided to be open to whoever could see me. I was even willing to drive to Seattle for therapy, which was over two hours away. I also wanted a female therapist because of the issues I had with my father.

None of the therapists responded to my many voicemails or emails for the longest time. Eventually, I found a therapist named William

E. Range in Port Townsend and left him a voicemail. He called me back that afternoon. When I spoke with him on the phone, he sounded kind and gentle, and we agreed on an appointment time. On my to-do list, I checked off "therapist."

At our first session, William said he had a few questions for me. Before he even asked one of them, I told him my story. After the fifty minutes were up, he said, "Wow. You've been through a lot. Good job. I'll see you next week." We met once a week for three years. He gave me three assignments: learn to journal, meditate, and practice mindfulness.

I read a book on meditation, and I began to meditate for an hour a day. Initially, I listened to guided meditations on YouTube focused on healing from narcissistic abuse and healing my inner child. Eventually, I was able to meditate on my own. Meditation and prayer taught me how to make peace with life moment by moment. Now I try to live my life in a state of meditation, and meditation has become a lifestyle.

While I had been a professional writer at the university for years, I had never kept a personal journal. In my notebooks, I wrote down my thoughts and any questions I had for my therapist. As a result of journaling, I learned to freely express my questions, hopes, fears, dreams, concerns, discoveries, and breakthroughs. Whenever I struggled with negative thoughts, which was all the time in the beginning, journaling helped me gain perspective by giving me distance and space between me and my thoughts. My journal entries provided much of the material for this book.

The family member who graciously cared for my mom while she was in hospice recommended I read anything I could by Byron Katie and Eckhart Tolle. As a result of their teachings, I learned everything I needed to know about living in the present moment and accepting life on its own terms. They challenged me to observe and question my thoughts. Both writers revolutionized my understanding of identity, faith, and life and strengthened my relationship with God. I learned not to take life and my thoughts so seriously. I also learned not to find my identity in anything outside myself. I stopped looking for external things and people to tell me I was OK.

The greatest lesson I learned in my recovery was always to be my authentic self and not to spend much time with people who didn't accept me just as I am. As much as I tried to make everyone around me happy, having this as a life goal only led to frustration, disappointment, unhappiness, and total exhaustion. Living a life where I loathed who I was while trying to please people also triggered my depression. Learning to accept my human imperfections and love my authentic self finally set me free.

As long as I focused on pleasing others, I was constantly adapting who I was to fit their needs, which is a miserable way to live. To succeed at being me, I need to be my authentic self at all costs, follow my heart, and only spend time with people who accept and respect me for me.

At the end of my three-year journey, I sold my home in Port Townsend, moved to Seattle to prepare this book for publication, and made plans to return to my home in Southern California. Many happy, loving, and joyful feelings I remembered as a child again flooded my heart. I was finally able to forgive myself. Over time, I was able to forgive my parents and come to terms with the loss of the love of my life.

Even though my dad couldn't express love to me through his life, he loved me the best he could despite his own toxic family wounds. I made the decision to forgive my father. I love you, Dad. My mom had been in a domestically violent relationship her entire adult life and just wanted to be loved. I made the decision to forgive my mother. I love you, Mom. Losing the love of my life will take me a lifetime to grieve. I miss him every day and will always love him.

I had lived my life not knowing who I was. Instead, I was pleasing people, isolating myself, and spending time with people and organizations that didn't even accept me. Because of the trauma I experienced in my toxic and abusive family and my feelings of shame and guilt regarding my sexuality, I felt uncomfortable in my own skin. I became codependent in my most intimate relationships, trying to please others because I could not please myself. I let other people run my life. I was reacting to what I thought other people wanted from me rather than following my own path. Giving over my power to other people is a miserable existence, and I'll never do that again.

Despite all my ups and downs, I've always felt like a higher power was watching out for me and taking care of me. Even in my darkest days, when I was among people who harmed me and did not accept me, I always received help from the kindness of strangers. My journey taught me we are all connected and everything happens for a reason. There are no mistakes in life. Everything that has happened to me has brought me to this perfect moment where I am enough and have everything I need.

I spent my life people-pleasing and looking for a place to belong until I realized life is about finding out who you really are. That's why scenery can change, relationships can come and go, and the heart can break over and over again and yet survive. I am finally free to listen to my heart, trust my intuition, and follow my dreams. I surrender to life. I have finally found my authentic voice. I am finally comfortable in my own skin.

LIVE YOUR AUTHENTIC LIFE

FORGIVE, MOVE ON & LET GO

Forgiving someone who hurt you is not easy. Letting go of the past and moving on from a traumatic relationship is difficult and doesn't happen overnight. As long as you live, you may never forget how your family harmed you, but you can still forgive them. For your own mental health and well-being, you need to forgive and let go of the pain, anger, and resentment you feel toward your family.

5 STEPS TO FORGIVE, LET GO & MOVE ON

Below are the five steps to forgive, let go, and move on:

- Step 1. Realize the consequences of unforgiveness.
- Step 2. Choose to forgive.
- Step 3. Understand that forgiveness doesn't mean reconciliation.
- Step 4: Let go of your anger.
- Step 5: Move on with your life.

STEP 1. REALIZE THE CONSEQUENCES OF UNFORGIVENESS.

Not forgiving your toxic family will probably hurt you more than it will hurt them. Chances are, they have no idea how much they hurt you. They may be blissfully unaware of how their toxic behavior harms everyone around them. Forgive for your sake. Forgive for your mental health. Forgive for your serenity and sanity.

Unforgiveness can lead to many powerful negative emotions as well as psychological and health problems:

166

- Anger
- Anxiety
- Bitterness
- Decreased immune response
- Depression
- Grudges
- Hatred
- Heart disease
- Increased blood pressure
- Increased heart rate
- Resentment
- Revenge
- Stress

STEP 2. CHOOSE TO FORGIVE.

Forgiveness is not a feeling but a conscious and intentional decision you must make. You must choose to forgive. You don't wake up one morning and feel like forgiving your toxic family. Forgiveness rarely happens on its own. Forgiveness is not a feeling. If you are waiting for your feelings to change before you forgive, you may be waiting a long time. Forgiveness is a decision and a choice. This is one of the reasons time does not heal toxic family wounds. You need to come to a place in your healing when you are ready to make a choice to forgive the people who hurt you the most.

Forgiveness is about deciding to let go of your resentment and your anger. You may not feel like forgiving them, but you can still choose to forgive. You may never forget what they did to you, but you can choose to let go of the resentment and anger for your own sake. Release the control the person has over you. Let go of wanting to seek revenge and justice or hold them accountable for their wrongdoing.

STEP 3. FORGIVENESS DOESN'T MEAN RECONCILIATION.

You can forgive your toxic family member and not reconcile with them or repair the relationship if you choose. If you have decided to walk away from a harmful family member, you forgive for your own sake. Forgiveness doesn't mean everything is all better now. Forgiveness is a decision you make for your healing. You can forgive someone and never see them again.

STEP 4: LET GO OF YOUR ANGER.

Siddhartha Buddha said, "Holding on to anger is like grasping a hot coal with the intent of throwing it at someone else; you are the one who gets burned." You will never heal your inner pain by holding onto your anger. Despite the pain and damage your family caused you, you must choose to forgive, let go, and move on for your own sake. There's no going back. Choose to live in the present moment and not the past. Choose to forgive and move forward with your life. You don't have to forget what happened, but you must stop allowing it to consume you.

Through therapy, journaling, meditation, and prayer, you can release your anger, bitterness, resentment, and grudges and, in your heart, say, "I forgive my toxic family; they have no idea how much they hurt me." Human beings make mistakes. You made mistakes too. It's time to let go.

STEP 5: MOVE ON WITH YOUR LIFE.

Stop reliving the hurt over and over in your mind and move on with your life. Build new relationships with accepting, safe, and supportive people. Participate in activities that make you happy and give you joy with people who accept you and care about you. Before joining new groups or making new friends, ensure you aren't repeating any toxic patterns you learned in your dysfunctional family relationships.

Sometimes you may need help moving on with a traumatic event. You may need professional help if you can't move past what happened in your toxic family. If you feel stuck in your past, it may be time to talk it out with a therapist.

Maybe you're not ready to forgive yet. Perhaps you need to hold onto your anger a bit longer. When you are ready, the choice is yours to make.

YOUR TOXIC FAMILY ISN'T YOUR FAULT

In the same way that abuse is not your fault, your toxic family is not your fault. How other people behave is never your fault, regardless of how many mistakes you made or how many things you wish you could change. Stop blaming yourself for what your toxic family did. When something goes wrong in life, it is human nature to want to assign blame. As a child, you may have blamed yourself when something went wrong in your toxic family. You may have continued this self-blaming pattern into adulthood.

Ask yourself these questions about mistakes you might have made in your toxic family:

- Even if you behaved perfectly, would your toxic family member still be harmful and dysfunctional?

- Are you confident that changing your behavior would have stopped your family members from reacting in a toxic manner to the world around them?

- If you could take yourself out of the equation, would your family members still be toxic?

- Did your toxic family members mistreat other people (relatives, neighbors, coworkers, service industry workers), and is that your fault too? Of course not.

Most toxic family members are toxic with everyone in their lives. You're not special. Whether a toxic family member mistreats everyone or singles you out for their abusive behavior, how another person behaves is never your fault and says nothing about who you are. Even if something you did upset them, it's still not your fault. They chose to respond to you in an unhealthy manner, which is not your fault because it is out of your control.

Even if you behaved perfectly around your toxic family members all of your life, you couldn't have changed their harmful behavior. Stop taking responsibility for what you cannot control. Even if your family members said, "This is all your fault," or, "You made me do this," you can't be responsible for another person's responses or actions. Your family members are toxic not because of you but because of their own unhealed trauma.

While you aren't perfect, you did nothing to deserve your family's abuse, neglect, and mistreatment. Even if you made a terrible mistake or did something irreparable, that does not allow your family the right to abuse you. If you are holding onto shame, guilt, or self-blame, you can let go whenever you are ready. It's time to let yourself off the hook for things you had no power to change or control. Don't let the mistakes of your family define who you are. Who you are is deeply profound, untouchable, and cannot be changed by anything or anyone. You must never allow anyone to define who you are or determine if you are OK. You are OK, just as you are, even if your toxic family is not.

LIVE YOUR AUTHENTIC LIFE

To survive your toxic family and reclaim your authentic life, you must be your authentic self at all costs, at all times, and in all relationships. You must accept life's complex plan and go with the flow of your life. Life always knows precisely what you need when you need it. Life knows the perfect ingredients for your authentic self to emerge and flourish. Accept yourself and accept life. Nothing happens by accident. Everything in life happens for a reason. You are part of something much bigger than yourself. The same life force that flows through you also flows through all of creation. Your authentic self is who you are at the core of your being. The energy flowing through you is your authentic life.

Being in harmony with all of life is essential to authentic self-expression. You will know you have achieved authenticity when everything you think, feel, and do, and all of your relationships, are in harmony with the essence of your true being. As a child, you may remember what love, joy, and happiness felt like before your family wounded you. Life was full of awe and wonder. You had hopes and dreams. The child you once were still exists within you as your authentic self. This child wants to play, love, have fun, and experience joy. Once dormant, your authentic self is now ready to emerge.

Authentic living leads to healthy, honest, open, and loving relationships which are not based on performance or a toxic family member's mood swings. You will find it difficult, if not impossible, to discover your authentic self while surrounded by unhealthy people who want to judge, shame, harm, or change you. These people prefer the people-pleasing mask-wearing version of you rather than the authentic self you were created to be. Walk away or keep a safe distance from anyone who doesn't accept, love, or allow you to be you, just as you are.

You don't need anyone's permission to be yourself. You don't need to wait for others to approve of you. You don't require anyone's validation. Boy George, from the London pop band Culture Club, gave excellent advice to a young singer on Australia's *The Voice*. He said, "Never look for acceptance from others. Your motto should always be, 'Take me as I am.'" You are OK, just as you are, even if everyone around you is not.

Your unhealthy family taught you a powerful lesson: for your health and well-being, you must only be in safe, supporting, and accepting relationships that encourage the full expression of your authentic self. When you are comfortable in your own skin and not dependent on others for approval or acceptance, you are free to live an authentic life. When you are at ease being yourself, life organically flows through you.

CHAPTER SEVEN SUMMARY

The final step to surviving your toxic family and reclaiming your life after toxic parents is to be your authentic self at all costs, at all times, and in all relationships. In this chapter, we explored how to forgive, move on, and let go, how your toxic family is not your fault, and the importance of living an authentic life without the negative influences of your toxic family.

CONCLUSION

—⟨❦⟩—

You now have the tools to find the strength, courage, and determination to face your pain, overcome dysfunctional family relationships, and live the authentic life you were born to live. You have learned to identify who you are underneath the grief your toxic family caused you. For some, that means keeping a distance between you and your dysfunctional family. For others, it may mean cutting ties with harmful family members forever.

Despite the chaos of your toxic family environment, you can strengthen your self-esteem and empower your true self by applying each chapter's fundamental principles in your daily life:

1. Your toxic family harmed you, but that doesn't mean you have to sit around and wait for them to keep harming you. Identifying your family's toxic characteristics is the first step toward healing and moving on with your life.

2. Learn healthy ways to manage and cope with your toxic family. You never have to spend another second with people who abuse and mistreat you. You never have to abuse your body or mind through self-medication to survive in a dysfunctional family.

3. Determine if your harmful family members are willing to change. If they are unwilling to change or cannot, walk away without looking back. You deserve a better life than the one your family gave you.

4. Set strong boundaries in your family relationships, letting people know how you want to be treated. Always remove toxic people from your inner circle. They gave up the right to have a close relationship with you long ago. You have the power to stop people from hurting you repeatedly. Take back your life!

5. Always take care of yourself first. Nobody can do that for you. Nobody in your toxic family is going to come and rescue you. You don't need to save your dysfunctional family either. You can be OK even if everyone around you is not.

6. Whenever you find yourself in mental distress, gain distance from your thoughts through journaling, meditation, or healthy self-care activities. Your identity—who you are—is separate and more important than the thoughts that run through your mind.

7. Be your authentic self always. Walk away from people and organizations who do not accept you exactly as you are. Forgive your toxic family and move on with your life. Don't waste another precious moment trying to make sense of why dysfunctional people do what they do—they don't even know.

Above all, never remain in a relationship where you are not respected or valued or where love harms you. Spend time with people who genuinely care for you and only want what's best for you. Find friends who make you feel comfortable, accept you as is, and love you for who you are. We are all connected. We all need help from others. Sharing your life with the right people is one of life's greatest pleasures. Spend time with people who don't expect you to be perfect and make it effortless for you to be yourself. Trying to be perfect is something you do around abusive and dysfunctional people, not in the real world.

You are in charge of your life. Don't ever give anyone that power over you. You are responsible for choosing who you keep close to you and setting healthy boundaries to protect your true self. Never wear a mask. Never be ashamed of who you are, which is a form of self-hatred. When you cannot be yourself around others, it's time to find others to be around. Always remember that nobody is perfect. To be human is to make mistakes. Embrace your imperfections, lean into them, and use them as tools on your journey toward personal growth and healing.

Always be honest with yourself. Deep down, you know who you are and what you want and need. Do not let anyone or anything limit you or your potential. Be your authentic self at all costs, at all times, and in all relationships. Sometimes people think they need to be the hero and prove their worth by helping others at their own expense. Be the hero of your own life, and don't waste your energy on undeserving people. See yourself for who you really are—a unique, beautiful soul—and allow nothing and no one to hold you back. Love people, but first, love yourself.

Carl Yung wrote, "The privilege of a lifetime is to become who you truly are." You don't have to change anything about yourself to be OK. Hang around people who celebrate you and make you feel more like yourself. Do what inspires you and what you have a passion for. Wherever you go, that's where you belong. Life is too short to live someone else's nightmare. Move on from your toxic family. Walk away from people who won't stop hurting you. Stay away from people who won't stop screwing with you.

Follow your heart, trust your intuition, and live the life of your dreams. You don't owe your life to anyone. You never did. Don't settle for less than you deserve. You deserve to be happy, not just

OK. You deserve joy, not just survival. You deserve a life triumphant, not just getting by. I wish you all the best on your healing journey. Embrace your life, as it is yours and yours alone. Don't be afraid to show the world what you're capable of. Unleash your amazing potential and light the world on fire.

Ite inflammate omnia. (Go forth, and set the world on fire.)
—ST. IGNATIUS OF LOYOLA

NOTE FROM THE AUTHOR

Did you find *The Toxic Family Solution* helpful? I would love to hear about your experience reading the book. Please take a moment to post a review on Amazon.com. I greatly appreciate your time and feedback. Best wishes and peace on your healing journey, Steven Todd Bryant.

ACKNOWLEDGMENTS

Thank you to my extended family for their support. Thanks to Dani Warnock and Jen Cabrera for supporting my return to full-time writing and crisis counseling. Thanks to Michael Seewer and Rev. Linzi Stahlecker at Saint Mark's Cathedral, Seattle, Jack Harlan at Peer Seattle, and Carol Wise at Coldwell Banker, Port Townsend for their tremendous support and assistance. A very special thanks to Byron Katie and Eckhart Tolle for their transformational teachings, which profoundly impacted my life. My deepest appreciation and gratitude go to Caleb Sheldrup, M. Psych. and William E. Range, MC, LMHC, for their advice, counseling, and expertise.

ACKNOWLEDGMENTS

About the Author

Steven Todd Bryant is the author of the therapist-recommended book, *The Toxic Family Solution*, a toxic family survivor, crisis counselor, and founder of ToxicFamily.org. He was on staff at the University of Southern California for 19 years and holds a BA in Communications and an MA in Theology. Connect with Steven at steventoddbryant.com.

Made in the USA
Las Vegas, NV
27 December 2023

83570750R00114